USING AN IMPACT MEASUREMENT SYSTEM TO EVALUATE LAND DEVELOPMENT

Philip S. Schaenman

The research for this report was made possible through a research grant from the Office of Policy Development and Research of the U.S. Department of Housing and Urban Development under the provisions of Section 701(b) of the Housing Act of 1954, as amended, to The Urban Institute. The publication of this report was supported in part by the Ford Foundation. The findings and conclusions presented in this report do not represent official policy of the Department of Housing and Urban Development, the Ford Foundation, or The Urban Institute.

THE URBAN INSTITUTE

Library of Congress Catalog Card Number 76-43199

U.I. 203-214-6

ISBN 87766-172-3

PLEASE REFER TO URI 15500 WHEN ORDERING

Available from:

Publications Office
The Urban Institute
2100 M Street, N.W.
Washington, D.C. 20037

List Price $3.95

Printed in the United States of America

First printing, September 1976

B/78/3M

FOREWORD

Three years ago, the U.S. Department of Housing and Urban Development contracted with The Urban Institute for a major survey of the methods which local governments might use to determine the economic, environmental, and social impacts of land development. With additional support from the Ford Foundation, a series of reports has been prepared covering virtually every aspect of impact analysis, from techniques and data adequacy to political problems associated with implementing an impact measurement system.

The first report in the series, *Measuring Impacts of Land Development: An Initial Approach,* described a comprehensive set of impact measures for assessing the effects of land use proposals. This report has been widely disseminated to federal, state, and local officials. On the basis of an independent survey of more than a thousand recent HUD-sponsored research projects, it was selected as being among the top ten percent that offered a high potential for improving local or state public services.

Four intervening reports have dealt intensively with fiscal, environmental, social, and private economic impacts. In *Fiscal Impacts of Land Development,* Thomas Muller examined the uses of fiscal studies, the state of the art presently used in making such studies, why findings in specific studies may differ, and what issues local officials should be alerted to when undertaking fiscal impact analyses. Dale Keyes, in *Land Development and the Natural Environment,* focused on data collection and analysis procedures, and the costs and reliability of techniques currently available for measuring impacts primarily on air and water, wildlife, vegetation, and noise. The effect of land use changes on employment, housing, and property values is the concern of *Economic Impacts of Land Development* by Thomas Muller. This report surveys the present state of the art, the costs of various estimating techniques, data sources, and the major analytical issues raised by previous studies. *Social Impacts of Land Development* by Kathleen Christensen describes an area of impact analysis which is in a much more rudimentary state of development, namely, how the perception and use of neighborhoods are influenced by changes in land use.

In this, the final report in the series, Philip Schaenman has pulled together what we have learned in the course of trying to implement an impact measurement system in local governments. Drawing on the experiences obtained from working directly with several local governments as well as the relevant findings in the preceding reports, Schaenman gives a comprehensive picture of the need for impact measurement, the practical state of the art, and the factors both facilitating and impeding the systematic use of impact analysis in land use decision making.

In this, as well as the other reports, the support and contribution of the project's Advisory Group was indispensible. And in this report in particular, the generous assistance of officials in Montgomery County, Maryland, Indianapolis, Indiana, and Phoenix, Arizona, which brought an element of practical understanding to the research team, must be given special acknowledgment.

The director of the Land Use Center, Worth Bateman and the Center's staff who conceived and worked on this series of reports should be proud of the contribution they have made. Nevertheless, they would be the first to point out that much remains to be done to bring a greater degree of rationality and informed judgment to land use decisions. Others will undoubtedly pick up where they have left off. It is our hope that this series provides a useful starting point.

William Gorham, *President*
The Urban Institute

iii

CONTENTS

EXHIBITS

ACKNOWLEDGMENTS

This study was sponsored by the Office of Policy Development and Research of the U.S. Department of Housing and Urban Development. The suggestions and encouragement of James Hoben, Allen Siegal, and Wyndham Clarke of this office are greatly appreciated.

The research was conducted under the general direction of Worth Bateman, executive director of The Urban Institute's Land Use Center. The study was initiated under Harry P. Hatry, director of the Institute's State and Local Government Research Program.

Dale Keyes, Tom Muller, and Kathleen Christensen of The Institute comprised the research staff for this project (in addition to the author who was project manager). They authored or coauthored the other reports in this series on evaluating impacts of land development. This report is based to a large extent on their findings. Their review of this report is also gratefully acknowledged.

Three local governments played an especially important role in this study by testing some of the suggested procedures and reviewing the concept in depth. We are especially appreciative of the participation and thoughtful comments and encouragement of Timothy A. Barrow, Mayor, and Richard F. Counts, Zoning Administrator, Phoenix, Arizona; F. Ross Vogelgesang, Director, and Gary Stair of the Division of Planning and Zoning, Indianapolis, Indiana; and Richard E. Tustian, Director, and staff members John Broda, Paula Gori, and Virginia Jones of the Montgomery County, Maryland, Planning Department. Many other staff members in these governments also made a contribution, for which we also wish to express our appreciation.

The Advisory Group (listed on page xi) provided some outstanding discussions of the issues of practical impact measurement and reviews for both this overview and the associated detailed reports. They were an exceptionally able group whose members actively participated in spite of personally hectic schedules.

Reviewers of the final draft included Charles Thurow, American Society of Planning Officials; Ronald Sendak, City of Falls Church, Virginia; and Samuel A. Finz, Fairfax County, Virginia.

Of course, the author takes full responsibility for this report and wishes to emphasize that specific suggestions and findings are not necessarily endorsed by any individuals, governments or groups above. There is considerable disagreement as to the best approach and level of effort appropriate for evaluating proposed land development. Except where a community is specifically referenced, the findings usually are based on the experience of several communities, and not necessarily just those of the governments which participated in this study.

ACKNOWLEDGMENTS

ADVISORY GROUP

TIMOTHY A. BARROW / *Mayor, Phoenix, Arizona*

KURT W. BAUER / *Executive Director, Southeast Wisconsin Regional Planning Commission, Waukesha, Wisconsin*

FRANK H. BEAL / *Director for Research, American Society of Planning Officials, Chicago, Illinois*

MELVIN L. BERGHEIM / *COUNCILMAN, Alexandria, Virginia, and National League of Cities-U.S. Conference of Mayors*

RICHARD F. COUNTS / *Zoning Administrator, Planning Department, Phoenix, Arizona*

CARL D. GOSLINE / *Director of General Planning, East Central Florida Regional Planning Council, Winter Park, Florida*

BERNARD D. GROSS / *Planning Consultant, Washington, D.C.*

HARRY P. HATRY / *Director, State and Local Government Research Program, The Urban Institute, Washington, D.C.*

TED KOLDERIE / *Executive Director, Citizens League, Minneapolis, Minnesota*

DENVER LINDLEY, JR. / *Commissioner, Bucks County, Doylestown, Pennsylvania*

JACK LINVILLE, JR. / *Deputy Executive Director, American Institute of Planners, Washington, D.C.*

ALAN H. MAGAZINE / *Supervisor, Fairfax County Board, Fairfax, Virginia, and Project Director, Contract Research Center, International City Management Association, Washington, D.C.*

ROBERT H. PASLAY / *Planning Director, Planning Commission, Nashville, Tennessee*

RICHARD A. PERSICO / *Executive Director, Adirondack Park Agency, Ray Brook, New York*

JAMES R. REID / *Director, Office of Comprehensive Planning, Fairfax County, Virginia*

E. JACK SCHOOP / *Chief Planner, California Coastal Zone Conservation Commission, San Francisco, California*

DUANE L. SEARLES / *Special Counsel on Growth and Environment, National Association of Home Builders, Washington, D.C.*

PHILIP A. STEDFAST / *Planning Director, Department of City Planning, Norfolk, Virginia*

DAVID L. TALBOTT / *Director of Planning, Falls Church, Virginia*

RICHARD E. TUSTIAN / *Director of Planning, Maryland National Capital Parks and Planning Commission, Silver Spring, Maryland*

F. ROSS VOGELGESANG / *Director, Division of Planning and Zoning, Indianapolis, Indiana*

THORNTON K. WARE / *Planning Director, Rensselaer County, Troy, New York*

JOSEPH S. WHOLEY / *Member, Arlington County Board, Arlington, Virginia, and Program Evaluation Studies Group, The Urban Institute, Washington, D.C.*

FRANKLIN C. WOOD / *Executive Director, Bucks County Planning Commission, Doylestown, Pennsylvania*

SUMMARY AND RECOMMENDATIONS

The fact that land use decisions significantly affect the quality of life both in the short and long run is now widely accepted by citizens and elected officials. Increased awareness of this has led many jurisdictions—urban and rural, large and small—to demand improved ways of evaluating the impacts of proposed and existing land development.

This report addresses that demand. It summarizes the results of a study aimed at improving procedures that cities, counties, and higher levels of government may use for evaluating land use changes—whether proposed private developments or changes stemming from public action such as comprehensive planning and zoning. The procedures also may be used for evaluating the impacts of previous development. It should be noted at the outset that many types of impacts are more appropriately considered in the context of general growth patterns, as discussed in work on comprehensive plans, rather than on the basis of one-by-one assessments of single developments.

The study considers practical ways to assess a broad range of impacts: on the local economy, the environment, public and private services, and on aesthetic, cultural, and social conditions of the community. Where possible, the impacts are described in terms of *end results to people* rather than in intermediate or technical terms. The procedures are intended to help governments comply with impact assessments required by federal and state laws, as well as for their own purposes.

The study accomplishes three major tasks:

- It identifies the state of the art of practical measurement procedures available to local (and other) governments for estimating various types of impacts.

- It sets forth an illustrative system of measures for assessing impacts of proposed development, identifying data collection and analysis procedures for each measure.

- It reflects initial testing of the measurement system undertaken with the cooperation of three communities: Phoenix, Arizona; Indianapolis/Marion County, Indiana; and Montgomery County, Maryland. The focus was on testing the system as a whole rather than on individual estimation methodologies. This experience provides insights on how to implement a measurement system, and certain advantages and disadvantages of the approach.

1

Valuable as the field testing was, it did not embrace the complete comprehensive approach described herein. Thus, results and data from the testing are inadequate to make a case that the impact measurement system described here definitely should or should not be recommended for detailed, quantitative analysis. Nevertheless, the system has seemed useful, at least for quick and qualitative reviews. The study has not succeeded in identifying the costs for all individual techniques or for the use of a system as a whole, partly because of the difficulty in identifying incremental evaluations that were conducted by existing government personnel with no extra ear-marked funds.

Problems associated with implementing the approach were generally greater than anticipated. Yet one community, Phoenix, felt that at least qualitative use of the system was inexpensive and useful, and is continuing to make some use of it.

Series of Reports and Intended Audiences

This report, one of a series of related reports, is intended primarily for planning directors and their staffs, planning commissions, and line agency personnel involved in development evaluation. It may also interest elected officials and citizens concerned with land use decisions.

Five other reports provide more detailed discussion of evaluation procedures for each measurement area.[1] The initial (1974) report, in the series, *Measuring Impacts of Land Development,* by Schaenman and Muller, has been superseded by this report and its companion pieces. Especially for readers familiar with that early report, it is referenced occasionally in this report to help identify what is new here.

Methodologies discussed in the five detailed reports can be used piecemeal, independent of whether a comprehensive evaluation approach is used. For example, a local government may gradually expand its repertory of measurement techniques according to the urgency and priority of the land use issues it is facing.

General Assessment of the Current Situation for Development Impact Evaluation

The current state of the art does not permit means of achieving practical estimations of many types of potential impacts of land development, including some of the more important types.

On the positive side, many governments are using increasingly sophisticated analytic techniques for evaluation. Moreover, considerable improvements appear well within reach even in the face of the shortages of money, staff time, and skills for evaluation purposes that commonly confront most governments.

Several critical elements seem necessary to assure that the state of the art is advanced. Among these are the following:

Education and dissemination

Decision makers, planning staff, other line agency staff, and citizens need further education about available methodologies and about the limitations of existing techniques. Better dissemination of existing practices, accompanied by candid explanations of what

---

1. Thomas Muller, *Fiscal Impacts of Land Development: A Critique of Methods and Review of Issues:*, Washington D.C., The Urban Institute, 1975; Thomas Muller, *Economic Impacts of Land Development: Employment, Housing, and Property Values,* Washington, D.C., The Urban Institute, 1976; Dale Keyes, *Land Development and the Natural Environment: Estimating Impacts,* Washington, D.C., The Urban Institute, 1976; Kathleen Christensen, *Social Impacts of Land Developments: An Initial Approach for Estimating Impacts on Neighborhood Usages and Perceptions,* Washington, D.C., The Urban Institute, 1976.

they can achieve, will help avoid the twin extremes of not expecting enough of planning staffs and of placing unrealistic demands upon them.

Research and testing

The development of better estimating tools, and further proving of existing ones, are needed for virtually every type of important impact. In light of the strong effects of local land use decisions on people's lives, the gap between the need for these tools and the research to obtain them is enormous. Emphasis should be placed on developing tools that governments may use without excessive cost or time.

Integration of planning and decision making

Making assessments and decisions on each specific land use proposal without reference to long-range plans makes little sense. It takes more time, and it runs up against legal constraints that would be minimized if a prior policy had been formulated to apply to all similar cases. Yet, logical as an integrated approach appears, it is difficult to attain. It requires that comprehensive plans, instead of sitting untouched on a shelf, should be analyzed and updated regularly, every five years at a minimum. It also requires that criteria used for judging specific projects be linked closely with comprehensive planning criteria.

Investments

One cannot ignore the pressures on local governments to reduce their expenditures. These pressures make it difficult to accomplish another requirement—a greater investment in the tools and staff used for estimating impacts. Though improvements seem feasible even with low funding, failure to make this kind of investment will probably retard public efforts to gain better control of community land use patterns.

Specific Findings

1. **An impact measurement system can be used in various ways by different users—it is a flexible concept, adaptable to many levels of staff resources and methodology.**

A measurement checklist such as suggested in Exhibit 3, page 27, can be used qualitatively if not quantitatively for most development decisions. It can also be used to evaluate comprehensive plans. Only a few measurements will be important in most development cases. Planning staff, planning directors, zoning administrators, planning commissioners, or citizens can use the measurements formally or informally. Any can use it independent of the others.

The use of checklists for qualitative or back-of-the-envelope estimates seems especially useful for reviewing small, non-precedent-setting developments and for zoning adjustments such as variances, special exceptions, or use permits. In the latter cases, a single individual may have both review and decision powers and can often identify the key issues without much formal analysis.

In-depth quantitative evaluation of individual proposed rezonings is much more expensive. It should be undertaken only for selected cases that are likely to be of special significance to the community. Even then, detailed analysis seems justified mainly to measure anticipated significant effects, to support claims that there will not be significant effects, or to avert or support court actions.

2. **Some types of impacts are better analyzed as part of comprehensive planning than for individual projects. Some are analyzable only as part of project reviews. However, all types of impacts should be at least briefly considered for each development.**

Impacts which, taken alone, have a relatively small effect on the whole community often fall into the first category; air and water quality effects of typical, several hundred unit suburban developments are examples. Highly localized impacts dependent on project details, such as those affecting neighborhood aesthetics or informal recreational opportunities, usually fall into the second category.

But the categories are not mutually exclusive; a development, for example, may generate *localized* air quality problems from its traffic and **areawide** aesthetic problems by blocking a cherished skyline.

3. **To make quantitative analysis of many impacts feasible, it is necessary to develop methodological tools and baseline data apart from the day-to-day decision process.**

It seems obvious that computer models and baseline physical measurements of air and water pollutant concentrations may be required for assessing impacts of new development on the natural environment. This approach is less often recognized and rarely undertaken for social impacts, however. Techniques such as periodic citizen surveys to assess citizen satisfaction with neighborhood conditions and to measure the usage of neighborhood facilities are available, practical, and desirable for improving estimates of social impacts.

4. **Many factors—technical, legal, political, institutional—may constrain the use of a comprehensive impact evaluation system by local government, especially for assessing proposed developments one-by-one.**

Technical constraints may be the most critical and reinforce the legal and institutional problems. There is a lack of methodologies that are sufficiently validated and practical for assessing certain impacts with adequate accuracy and confidence. This does not obviate the need for qualitative use of the measures, but it makes it more difficult to defend the results legally, and may be so intellectually unsatisfying to analysts that they are unwilling to use them.

Legal constraints may eliminate certain factors from being used as reasons for rejecting development proposals, or even from general consideration. These constraints usually apply less to planned unit developments (PUDs) than other rezonings. Legal constraints vary from state to state, by type (variances, special exceptions, and other zoning adjustments) and by stage of decision process (e.g., hearing, appeal). But even measures that may not be used as direct criteria can identify potential impacts to bring citizen or developer pressures to bear and thus influence outcomes, or to identify areas for "trading" of amenities or ameliorating features in return for relaxation of other constraints such as floor-to-area ratios.

Political and institutional constraints include commissions or citizenry with strong pro- or anti-development biases that are thought unlikely to be swayed by comprehensive or detailed impact information. Yet reliance on "political" considerations may in fact result from a lack of reliable and objective information.

In spite of these barriers, application of a comprehensive evaluation system appears valuable for many communities, even if used only internally by the planning staff.

5. **Most communities rarely if ever undertake retrospective evaluations.**

This eliminates a crucial type of feedback needed for decision making: most communities are continually making predictions about development impacts, but not testing their accuracy. Retrospective evaluations also are needed as case studies which can be used to help estimate social impacts of proposed development where models are lacking. Analogies provide a useful adjunct from which to infer impacts.

6. **The state of the art for assessing various impacts is middling in most cases—not as good as many think in some areas but better than suspected in others. All areas need improvement, all permit some progress.**

What superficially seems to be a sharp grouping of solid, scientific methodologies on one hand (e.g., for pollution impacts) and soft, purely judgmental methods on the other (e.g., for assessing aesthetic and social impacts) is not supported by more detailed examination. Many air and water quality computerized models, for example, have not been validated and even the better ones still require judgments to be made as to allowable concentrations of pollutants in the absence of conclusive evidence on health and annoyance thresholds, although federal standards are of considerable assistance.

On the other hand, citizen surveys, direct observations by trained observers, and visual simulations seem to provide the potential for reaching considerably better estimates of aesthetic and social impacts than are generally realized to date.

7. **The potential advantages and disadvantages of using a system of measures for evaluating proposed land development include the following:**

Advantages

- *Comprehensiveness.* Major impacts often stand out, getting quickly identified in most types of evaluations. Besides helping to ensure that these big impacts are not overlooked, the comprehensive approach helps identify less obvious but important impacts by requiring all aspects to be explicitly considered. The focus on "end impacts" also encourages thinking through implications of intermediate changes.

- *Consistency and fairness.* Using a measurement list as a starting point for each evaluation can help reduce differences in evaluations from staff member to staff member. Local governments are thus less susceptible to charges of inconsistent treatment than when ad hoc evaluations are used. Consistency in measures and terminology also can make it easier to compare data from different evaluations, and to use case histories for estimating impacts.

- *Clarity.* The explicit listing of measures used in evaluation, and the repeated use from case to case, should help all parties better understand the basis for decision making in advance. The emphasis on quantification helps clarify the magnitude of various impacts. The emphasis on end impacts from the citizens' view helps ensure the relevancy of the evaluation; it also reduces the chances of misunderstandings that may result from different interpretations of the changes in intermediate factors such as traffic volumes or population density.

- *Increased awareness.* Elected officials, planning commissioners and citizens can be made more aware of the complexities and possible ramifications of development by being given a checklist of measures and perhaps even associated information on data collection procedures. This can also lead to greater appreciation of the need for impact evaluation and a more knowledgeable dialogue among parties to land use decisions.

- *Improved defense of decisions.* Presumably a more comprehensive, clearer set of decision criteria should help decision makers explain and defend decisions, making it easier to demonstrate that a thorough, rational, fair, and consistent approach was used.

- *Identification of gaps in local tools, expertise, or data.* The process of preparing for use of a measurement system helps identify gaps in analytical tools and data needed for evaluation. It prods those adopting the system to find out in detail who knows what and who has which tools in various departments. This benefit accrues regardless of whether the system is actually implemented.

- *Training new staff and commission members.* The measurement system provides a description of the evaluation process which can be helpful in training new planning staff or commission staff members and assuring continuity of approach. This is especially important in governments with high staff turnover.

- *Common language.* If used both for reviewing projects and evaluating plans, the measurement system provides a basis for improving communications and cooperation between the project review and comprehensive planning parts of the planning department, and between the planning department and line agencies.

Disadvantages[2]

- *Small incremental improvement.* In some communities, the system may not add a sufficient amount of new information to influence decision making, either because the staff is currently doing as good an evaluation job as possible under local legal and other constraints, or because the decision making body is not likely to heed such information due to rigid political biases or lack of adequate training.

- *Slower decisions, higher costs.* A more detailed impact evaluation can lengthen the time needed before decisions can be made and may increase costs of decision making for developers and the government, especially when the system is first used. On the other hand, recent evidence indicates these costs are modest, and incurring them ultimately may reduce net time by not requiring the development of an ad hoc approach for each case.

---

2. See, also, item 4 above about constraints on usage.

- *Vulnerability of decisions.* Increased challenges to land use decisions, in or out of courts, may result from having a clearer target to shoot at, especially for measures that do not have strong scientific methodology behind them yet.

- *Rigidity.* Commission, courts, or citizens might insist that analysis be made in detail for every (or too many) developments once it is done on one. This also applies to ad hoc approaches, though perhaps less obviously. The measurements might also lead to the exclusion of nonquantifiable impacts—but this would be an incorrect application.

- *Implied accuracy.* The use of impact measurements as a whole may suggest a level of accuracy that is not within the current state of the art, (although the intent is the opposite—to clarify what is and is not known about potential impacts).

Recommendations to Local Governments and Regional Agencies

1. **Determine if a comprehensive evaluation system is appropriate for your jurisdiction.**

Identify local objectives in land use planning and formulate a set of related impact measures, perhaps using those suggested in Exhibit 3 as a starting point. Apply them to a few test cases, at least qualitatively. Assess the capability for providing the necessary data, and local constraints on usage. The process can yield side benefits such as identifying needs for improving information and clarifying the existing review process, even if a measurement system does not get adopted explicitly.

2. **In using an impact measurement checklist, briefly scan the list for each proposed development, but be selective in undertaking in-depth analyses of any measure.**

This is the only practical way to use the measures. Virtually no local government has the resources to do in-depth analysis on every measurement, and it would be wasteful to do so in any event. Qualitative, judgmental estimates can suffice for most measures, but the way the estimates are reached and some indication of their accuracy should be indicated. And "sensitivity analyses," which show how much an estimated impact might vary as the assumptions behind it vary, should be used where there is considerable uncertainty about the assumptions and where the decision might change for different, equally plausible assumptions.

3. **Estimated impacts of proposed land development should be disaggregated when appropriate by clientele groups, such as: neighborhood areas, developers and other business interests, and low-income families.**

By disaggregating estimated impacts by clientele groups, there is less chance that significant impacts will be lost sight of in community-wide averages. Who will benefit and who will lose from the the proposal will be more clearly identified.

4. **Consider use of the same measurement system for project reviews and evaluation of comprehensive plans.**

Linkages between the two processes often need strengthening, and this is one mechanism toward that end. Also, large development proposals are often plans for a substantial part of a community, and dull the boundary between project reviews and planning.

5. **Consider improving data collection and analysis methodologies for estimating specific types of impacts (e.g., wildlife abundance, air pollution, fiscal flows) even if a comprehensive measurement system is not to be used.**

The reports in this series, listed in footnote 1, describe the state of the art available to local governments.

6. **If comprehensive plans are not updated frequently, say once every five years, periodic analysis of the cumulative effects of development to date, and the potential cumulative effects of proposed or expected development should be considered.**

Outdated plans may be based on assumptions that no longer hold, such as the per capita auto usage or the pollutant levels considered hazardous. Old plans also may have neglected certain impacts due to a lack of staff resources at the time, or because of political compromises that no longer have relevance.

It may be advisable, therefore, to assess periodically the areawide cumulative effects of development to date (perhaps in terms of the "preferred" measures in Exhibit 3) to see if compliance with the comprehensive plans suffice as a guide for assessing further development.

7. Consider the inclusion of "targets" for certain types of impacts in comprehensive plans.

Maximum acceptable targets could be devised for such things as traffic volume, pollution levels, storm drainage run-off, or flooding incidence. Corresponding to these targets could be tipping points or thresholds for some intermediate or contributing factors, such as numbers of housing units, square feet of office space, or acreage of impermeable ground cover. Estimates of these factors would permit simple running counts to be kept until a tipping point was reached; that would trigger a more detailed analysis. This approach allows cumulative effects to be assessed without necessitating detailed analyses for every new project. Further, the implications of comprehensive plans become more specific and clear once the targets are set.

8. Weighting systems to "add up" impacts of different types are more likely to confuse than clarify. It is recommended that local and regional governments avoid the use of such weighting systems.

Findings from the use of a set of impact measures do not automatically tell whether a development should be denied, approved, or approved with modifications. This is a matter of judgment, involving tradeoffs between plus and minus factors. If all the factors are combined in a weighted index, the bases for judgment are hidden from view. So even if a measurable set of weights could be assigned to each measure and each range of values (which is doubtful), it seems preferable to let decision makers see the full set of pros and cons in the context of each decision. Their job, in essence, is to do the weighting themselves.

9. More attention needs to be paid, on one hand, to educating appointed and elected decision makers on types of impacts and their interpretation, and on the other hand, to educating the technicians to improve the clarity of language and formats used to present impact information to the decision makers.

Many decision makers serve only part time, and are not technically trained. There is no point in improving the scope and quality of information if it will not be used—yet that seems to be a major source of frustration for many planning agencies.

10. Use of trained observers and citizen surveys should be considered as means of periodically assessing how citizens utilize their neighborhoods and how satisfied they are with various aspects of these neighborhoods.

Data obtained from such observations and surveys can be accumulated as baseline information to aid in planning and in estimating the kinds of changes to expect from specific development proposals. This would be especially useful for community areas that are currently undergoing change or where change is anticipated. The collected data would enable retrospective studies to be carried out, after development occurs, to portray neighborhood impacts. The data would also serve as a check against the representativeness of citizen feedback at public hearings.

I. INTRODUCTION

There is undoubtedly wide agreement on the need for heightened awareness and better understanding of the impacts of land development—both the positive and negative impacts.[1] Land development is a vital issue on the front pages, in the courts, and in neighborhood conversations.

Local governments especially bear the brunt of decision making authority and pressures. Regional, state, and federal agencies also are clearly interested in improved ways to evaluate proposed plans and specific developments. So are potentially affected citizens, individually and in groups. Then why is there still so much use of ad hoc approaches to development evaluation? Why is there a lack of more systematic approaches, such as the comprehensive set of impact measurements discussed in this report? Why is so little of the available methodology in use?

There are good explanations for this situation. The current state of the art of evaluation tools falls far short of local government needs for assessing many types of impacts, once you look under the covers of the jargon or computer models. Local government staffs often are not adequately sized, or staffed with the necessary expertise, or given the necessary time to undertake desired analyses.

The private development community voices concern that additional evaluations may delay projects, increase costs to the public, force the small developer out, and, to compound matters, not really add much of importance to the accuracy or fairness of the evaluation.[2]

Admittedly the task is complex—because land development affects so much of life and so many power groups. Nevertheless, it appears that considerable improvement can be achieved now by governments of all sizes, even in light of tight budgets.

---

1. "Impacts" in much of the current literature are taken to mean only negative effects, such as detrimental effects on the environment. This is an unbalanced view and obscures one reason that land use decisions often are so complex and difficult. It needs to be stressed that development also may have positive impacts—more jobs, new homes, elimination of eyesores, industrial growth, and so forth.

2. Note, however, that costs of preparing Environmental Impact Statements (EIS) in California in 1974 were estimated by developers and consultants at $4–10,000 a development or $10–25 per housing unit; plus public sector costs of $2,000 per application or $4–25 per unit. Somewhat higher private sector costs per unit and somewhat lower public costs per unit were estimated for EIS preparations for developments of regional impact in Florida. For further discussion of costs, delays, and usage of state-required impact evaluations, see, T. Muller and K. Christensen, *State-Mandated Impact Evaluation: Preliminary Assessment,* contract report to U.S. Department of Housing and Urban Development, Washington, D.C., 1976.

SCOPE AND PURPOSE

This report summarizes a HUD-sponsored study to identify and further develop practical procedures for evaluating impacts of land development.[3] Emphasis here is on impacts on the community and its citizens rather than on the adequacy of sites for development or the effects of developments on their potential users.

There are three major thrusts to the study:

- An overview of the state of the art of techniques for assessing economic, natural environment, aesthetic, social, and public service impacts of development.
- The development of a system of impact measurements and associated data collection and analysis methods for evaluating development.
- Partial testing of the measurement system approach with the help of three local governments—Phoenix, Indianapolis, and Montgomery County, Maryland.

The emphasis was on methods for evaluating individual development proposals—which is the way a great many land use decisions are made. But most of the discussion also applies to evaluating land use plans and cumulative effects of development.

Evaluation may be conceived as obtaining and analyzing information on potential impacts, then using the results to help make decisions. This study and report deals with improving the information authorizing and analysis procedures, and how the procedures might be worked into the existing decisionmaking process. The administrative parts of the decision process are beyond the scope of this study; this is not for lack of importance; in fact, some believe that improving the decision process is more likely to satisfy affected citizens than is better information.

An impact measurement system is another tool for use in the decision process. It is complementary to code enforcement, informal negotiations, public hearings, and appeals. As an information device, it aids decision makers but is not a decision making tool.

The viewpoint here is neither for nor against development or growth. But the fact is that most proposed land developments get approved unless staff or citizens show compelling reasons not to approve them. Encouraging more review therefore may have an inherent bias toward making development approvals more difficult. However, the proposed procedures are intended to improve the fairness and rationality of decision making by identifying both positive and negative impacts of development.

Intended Audience and Relation to Other Reports in Series

This report is primarily intended for planning directors and their staffs, and line agency personnel who help evaluate impacts. Planning commissions, members and other participants in land use decision making may also be interested.

Initial ideas on an impact evaluation system, presented in an earlier report[4] undergo a number of revisions in this report. The changes are based on limited testing in three communities, extensive discussion with our Advisory Group, and additional research.

A series of other reports from this project offers more detail on available procedures and analysis issues in assessing various types of impacts. They are as follows:

---

3. Another recent HUD-sponsored study takes a somewhat different but complementary approach toward evaluating land development proposals. It is described in *Interim Guide for Environmental Assessment,* Field Office Edition, Final Report No. H-2080R, prepared for the U.S. Department Housing and Urban Development, 1975.

4. Philip S. Schaenman and Thomas Muller, *Measuring Impacts of Land Development,* Washington, D.C., The Urban Institute, 1974.

Economic Impacts

1. Thomas Muller, *Fiscal Impacts of Land Development: A Critique of Methods and Review of Issues,* 1975.
2. Thomas Muller, *Economic Impacts of Land Development: Employment, Housing, and Property Values,* The Urban Institute, 1976.

Natural Environment Impacts

3. Dale Keyes, *Land Development and the Natural Environment: Estimating Impacts,* The Urban Institute, 1976.

Social Impacts

4. Kathleen Christensen, *Social Impacts of Land Development: An Initial Approach for Estimating Impacts on Neighborhood Usages and Perceptions,* The Urban Institute, 1976.

These detailed reports are intended for a somewhat more specialized audience—especially planning staff responsible for estimating specific types of impacts—but many parts of them should be relevant and undertandable to a more generalized audience.

Each report is self-standing and somewhat unique in character, reflecting differences in the state of the art in each area. The fiscal and natural environment reports describe and evaluate existing methodologies in these heavily researched fields. The social impacts report is at the other extreme; it suggests a largely untested approach for an elusive, underresearched area. It emphasizes an integrated approach to assessing neighborhood social impacts and therefore includes some environmental and services impacts also discussed in others in the series.

The social impacts report slightly overlaps some of the other impact areas in order to stress the importance of considering combinations of neighborhood impacts together.

It is hoped that this series of reports will stimulate local governments to improve their own ways of evaluating land developments and plans. Many of the procedures discussed also apply to meeting requirements of federal and state environmental impact statements. Finally, it should be noted that the series is not a set of all-inclusive cookbooks. They cover a broad range of impacts and aim to deal with those of most widespread interest, but certainly not all potentially important impacts for every community.

TERMS AND EMPHASES[5]

Land development refers to a significant change in the kind or intensity of use of a site. The main thrust of this study deals with land use changes that require government approval, such as rezonings, variances, or special exceptions. Much of the discussion here and in other reports in this series applies to reviewing comprehensive, sector, area, or neighborhood plans as well. The scale of development to be evaluated may range from a single highrise structure to the reshaping of a major portion of a community.

Private Sector Emphasis

This report is oriented to development initiated by the private sector, although the measures presented there generally may be applied to public sector land development as well. In the

---

5. These are consistent with the initial report and others in the series.

latter case, additional measures would be needed for facilities such as hospitals and fire stations to more fully reflect their likely impact on service quality.

Clientele Groups

The suggested measures are intended to reflect the concerns of citizens. All citizens, however, are not affected in the same way, or in the same degree, by particular developments. Therefore, besides looking at impacts on the community as a whole, it is advisable to estimate explicitly the impacts on different population segments—such as citizens living near the proposed development, the businessmen affected, low-income groups, and visitors. Unless this is done, the most articulate and aggressive groups may wield disproportionate influence to the detriment of others who have an equally legitimate stake in the community's future. (See Chapter IV.)

Impact Measures

Impact measures are the standards—like yardsticks or thermometers—against which effects of development are gauged.

Impact Measurements

Impact measurements are like the inches on a yardstick or the degrees of temperature on a thermometer. They are the quantitative expression of the measures that reflect effects of development. They are physically or statistically measured for establishing baseline conditions when used in before-and-after studies. For proposed development, the measurements have to be forecast. When the measurements cannot be calculated precisely, they may be expressed qualitatively, such as "modest effect," "apparently great effect."

Procedures

Measurement procedures or estimation procedures indicate the way data are to be collected and analyzed for identifying impacts.

Areas of Impact

Impact areas are community, neighborhood, or household attributes or classes of attributes that can be affected by development. Examples are employment, air quality, recreational opportunity, and privacy. Sometimes the more general categories such as local economy, natural environment, or social conditions are also called impact areas.

BACKGROUND

An exploratory project in 1972 led to the initial report[6] and findings that few if any local governments were routinely using a documented checklist of impact measures for evaluating developments. Those conducting impact evaluations generally had to make up procedures as they went along. Not a single published document could be found at the time that discussed a comprehensive approach to impact evaluation in more than superficial terms. Most reports that did discuss procedures for evaluating impacts were limited to a single type of impact (e.g., fiscal flow, noise, or traffic volumes).[7] It was decided, therefore, to develop a compre-

---

6. Schaenman and Muller, *Measuring Impacts of Land Development,* op. cit.

7. This has changed somewhat in the last few years. See, for example, *Interim Guide for Environmental Assessment,* op. cit. Reports which summarize models available for assessing environmental and transportation impacts are cited in the detailed reports in this Urban Institute series.

hensive checklist of impact measures and to suggest appropriate estimating procedures for each measure.

Two local governments—Indianapolis, Indiana and Montgomery County, Maryland—agreed to assist in testing the checklist and related procedures that were devised. Later, Phoenix, Arizona also volunteered to undertake testing and made important contributions.

An Advisory Group consisting of local and regional government planners and elected officials, and of representatives of professional planning societies, citizen groups, and the private development community played a major role in guiding the project and reviewing its products.[8]

THE NEED FOR A SYSTEMATIC APPROACH TOWARD MEASURING IMPACTS

Current evaluations of proposed land development by local government often have one or more of the following shortcomings:

Lack of Comprehensiveness.

Important impacts are often ignored. Sometimes these omissions occur simply because of the lack of a systematic approach. Certain items may be ignored regularly due to tacit assumptions about what is appropriate to consider. Some omissions are due to state or local legal constraints on types of impacts that may be considered as a basis for ruling on a proposal. Some omissions are due to lack of staff time or expertise for a making certain estimates. Noise, informal recreational use of neighborhood space, privacy, and effects on land values are examples of impact areas which are frequently ignored.

Lack of Consistency

A development may get reviewed in entirely different ways depending on which staff member is in charge. What gets considered is often heavily influenced by the data the developer happens to provide and what the planning commission, council members, or court examiners request. While a rigid approach can lead to wasteful analyses, the lack of a consistent framework for evaluation also can lead to numerous problems, including:

- Unfairness to various parties as evaluation priorities change from case to case.[9]

- Difficulties in communication among the parties to the decision because the definitions and methods for evaluation keep changing.

- Uncertainty and apprehension among the parties regarding how the evaluation will be done and what data needs to be collected.

Lack of Clarity

Much of the evaluation dialogue traditionally is in technical terms (e.g., FARs or floor-area ratios, and pollutant levels) which are difficult to understand by citizens as well as some decision makers, or intermediate measures (e.g., persons per acre, vehicles per hour, acres of park per capita) which seem clear but whose interpretation depends on a chain of assumptions that may not be clear even to "experts." The evaluation dialogue also uses terms that sound

---

8. The Advisory Group members are listed on page xi.

9. Developers especially have a stake in consistent evaluations. Uncertainties in decision making processes may increase business risks and costs to customers. In Indianapolis, local builders specifically asked the director of planning and zoning to provide a checklist to be used in subdivision evaluations to eliminate some of the uncertainties.

meaningful but are hard to pin down, such as character of neighborhood, urban sprawl, or neighborhood stability.

The measures and procedures offered in this series of reports are intended to help alleviate these shortcomings by providing a way to describe impacts on the citizens more explicitly, systematically, and comprehensively, and in reasonably nontechnical terms. Any set of practical measures is obviously unlikely to be satisfactory on all these scores, but there seems to be enough chance to advance toward the goal for most governments to warrant the effort.

ORGANIZATION OF THE REPORT

The framework and assumptions behind the use of the suggested impact measurement system are discussed in Chapter II. A suggested set of impact measures and associated data collection procedures is presented in Chapter III. Clientele groups that may be affected differently by development are discussed in Chapter IV. The state of the art of data collection procedures and the needed baseline data are summarized in Chapter V. Chapter VI discusses ways to use the measurement system, constraints to its use, and some general analysis issues to be kept in mind. Chapter VII provides examples of use of the measures. Chapter VIII outlines how a jurisdiction determines whether to use the system, and how to get started. Chapter IX concludes with an assessment of the approach by local governments that have had some experience with it.

II. ASSUMPTIONS AND EVALUATION APPROACHES

The suggested approach for evaluating land development proposals stems chiefly from the apparent deficiencies in current procedures used by local and other levels of governments, noted in the preceding chapter, plus a few general observations and assumptions about the nature of land use decisions. The assumptions are *not* as obviously sound as they may appear at a glance, nor is the suggested approach necessarily an improvement. The simplistic application of a set of measures is no guarantee of better decisions; it can even obscure nonquantified or nonquantifiable issues.

The proper use of measurements in the right environment, however, does seem to have potential for improving decision making. The assumptions and general approach are outlined below. The environment that seems necessary for successful application is discussed in Chapters VI and VIII.

ASSUMPTIONS ABOUT DEVELOPMENT REVIEW

1. *Better decisions can be made if the various parties involved in land use decisions have a clear understanding of the likely impacts of development.*

Clarity requires information to be presented with a minimum of jargon, in terms likely to be understood by citizens and decision makers. The information should be clearly displayed and documented. All likely significant impacts should be flagged.

The assumption also implies that impact measures should focus on "end" effects on citizens or on changes to community objectives. Focusing on intermediate variables makes interpretation of the effect of citizens' welfare unclear.[1]

This is not to imply that "end impacts" are easily pinpointed or measured. At an extreme, the only end impacts might be said to be health and happiness. But these ends are so highly aggregated as to be almost abstract, and one usually cannot translate concrete, detailed results of development into such terms. The bases for comparisons among alternative developments and remedial action need to be more specifically defined. This calls for selecting particular measures that are sufficiently end-oriented to be meaningful and workable within present knowledge. (Suggested measures are presented in Chapter III.) For example, we may settle today for a measure such as "change in air pollution concentrations, and the number of people affected (by health or nuisance problems)" because a more preferable measure, "change in average life expectancy or episodes of illness due to air pollution," is too difficult to estimate. Even

---

1. Arguments at citizen hearings often result from poor translations of intermediate variables by various parties. For example, an increase of traffic by 40 vehicles per hour above an existing 40 per hour may be visualized differently by various citizens because of a lack of feel for numbers or for how that magnitude translates. If related in terms of noise change in residential area, traffic congestion, or safety hazards, the issue might be more readily visualized and resolved.

in that framework, the measure used may achieve different levels of refinement. Just stating the expected parts per million of a pollutant is least desirable. It is better to indicate the number of persons living in an area where federal or state pollution limits are exceeded. Even better is to estimate the number living in an area where standards will be exceeded x times per year at an intensity likely to trigger or exacerbate symptoms in people with breathing difficulties, and so forth. This measure could be further disaggregated to specify how many elderly will be affected, since they are presumably more susceptible than others to these health difficulties.

Another complexity is deciding whether end results deal with citizens' perceptions, or changes in physical conditions. For example, are newly created sightlines from an apartment building into people's backyards the end impacts, or are perceived reductions of privacy the ends? To avoid getting lost in a philosophical morass, we suggest measures to reflect changes in *both* the physical conditions and perceptions, where both can be used. Since we usually cannot directly predict the latter, one must turn to knowledge of how people have reacted to similar physical changes in the past.

Having more and clearer information available does not guarantee improved decisions. To obtain good data and analysis may prolong the time to make a decision. The findings also may open up new fields of disagreement among various interest groups—perhaps without resolving the issues. Increased information thus may be viewed by some as an attempt by government to overload and confuse the interested parties.

Despite these possible roadblocks, informed impact evaluations may shoot down bogeymen, get discussions focused on the relevant issues, and encourage an openness in decision making. This openness, along with improved access and quality of citizen participation in the land use process, is a potential antidote for the dangerous alienation toward government prevalent today. Like most tools, an impact measurement system can be used properly or improperly.

2. *A development usually has multiple impacts; a few are usually more important than the rest; but which ones are important vary from case to case.*

This explains the desirability of giving at least initial consideration to a broad range of potential impacts—economic, environmental, aesthetic, social, and public service quality—to help ensure that the most important ones are not overlooked. It also suggests why it is difficult to select a fixed set of weights for converting the various types of impacts into a common scale.

That a great variety of issues are likely to arise in particular cases was borne out by a content analysis of newspaper articles about rezonings which took place in the course of one year in the New York City, Washington, D.C., and San Francisco areas, as displayed in Exhibit 1. The need for a broad set of measures was also suggested by reviews of initial checklists by Indianapolis, Montgomery County, Maryland, and Phoenix planning departments and by the project Advisory Group. It seems difficult to reduce a checklist to fewer than about 28 or 30 impact areas with nearly 50 measured attributes within these areas. For virtually every one of these areas, examples of specific developments can be cited where it was a major consideration.

3. *Only a small subset of impact measures are likely to require detailed consideration, in most cases.*

Only the relatively few large or precedent-setting developments are likely to require detailed analysis of many measures. Most proposed developments individually will have only localized effects that are small and non-crucial and these usually do not require elaborate analyses. If the suggested approach required detailed study of many measures it would be prohibitively expensive and time consuming. (However, the cumulative effects of small developments, while often very significant, are hard to deal with, as discussed in Chapters V and VI.)

During an initial testing of a proposed checklist of 48 measures in Phoenix, it was noted that a proposed development typically raises issues involving six to eight measures; only rarely are a third or more of the measures involved. None of the proposed developments reviewed required more than that.[2]

---

2. Personal communication from Richard Counts, Zoning Administrator, Phoenix, Arizona, June 2, 1975.

EXHIBIT 1
FREQUENCY OF MAJOR ISSUES IN DEVELOPMENT REVIEWS

Issues	Number of Cases in Which Issue Was Raised			
	Washington D.C. Area	New York City Area	San Francisco Area	Total
I. *Economic Impacts*				
Property value and rents	3	2	0	5
Effect on public finances and other budgetary issues	5	5	3	13
Employment	0	1	1	2
Equitable distribution of economic benefits or penalties	1	5	0	6
Neighborhood or regional economy	0	2	1	3
Economic viability of the development	0	0	2	2
II. *Natural Environment Impacts*				
Greenery	3	1	3	7
Ecological effects	5	1	3	9
III. *Aesthetic and Cultural Impacts*				
Aesthetics and views	8	9	9	26
Historic and cultural values	3	0	2	5
IV. *Socio-Political Impacts*				
Mixture of people	0	8	1	9
Sociability	1	1	1	3
Loss of privacy	1	0	0	1
Displacement of occupants	2	4	0	6
Quality of housing	1	3	0	4
Housing variety	0	3	0	3
Community control	0	1	1	2
Density	1	3	0	4
V. *Public Service Impacts*				
Traffic-related issues	4	4	2	10
Safety	1	3	3	7
Other public services	4	3	2	9
VI. *General*				
Growth trends	5	6	3	14
Owner's freedom to use land	0	2	0	2
"Character of my neighborhood"	0	0	2	2

NOTES: Adapted from Exhibit 1-A in P. S. Schaenman, et al., "Measuring Impacts of Land Development," Working Paper 201-8, Appendix A, The Urban Institute, 1972. It is based on a content analysis of all cases written up in the *Washington Post*, 3/1/72–6/15/72; the *San Francisco Examiner* and *San Francisco Chronicle*, 7/1/70–2/28/71; and a sample of cases in the *New York Times*, 1/70–3/72. The cases analyzed numbered 15 in Washington, 19 in New York, 12 in San Francisco, and a total of 46.

Most cases involve several key issues: therefore the sum of the columns is greater than the number of cases. Although some issues raised could fall into more than one category, they are recorded under what seemed the most relevant category. Classifying primary issues required some interpretation where articles were not totally explicit.

Assumptions and Evaluation Approaches

4. *The various impact areas (economic, service quality, natural environment, social) are strongly interrelated.*

Economic effects such as changes in employment may have social impacts. Changes in fiscal flows may affect the quality of public services that can be afforded. Chains of effects may occur as when development alters the natural environment, which reduces aesthetic appeal, which affects land values, which curtails property tax revenues, which decreases the monies available to localities for ameliorating or controlling the changes to the natural environment.

These interrelationships imply that impact analysis should be self-consistent, using the same assumptions in analysis of various impact areas. For example, the range of estimated changes in the number of automobile trips should be the same for assessing impacts on air pollution, noise, social conditions, and transportation. Fiscal flows should not be computed using current average per capita public service expenditures from the existing community while at the same time the new development is assumed to require considerably more or less public services than the rest of the community. Since technical analyses are often prepared by staff in various line departments outside the planning and zoning administration, close coordination is needed to prevent inconsistencies. This must be ensured by the person in charge of the development review.

A second implication is the need to consider impacts comprehensively, not only initially, but also after the drafting of development plan revisions. This should help guard against tailoring a development to look good from the viewpoint of some measures without regard to others. For example, a neighborhood parking shortage discovered in the initial impact analysis might be remedied by replacing some open space with additional parking—but this may affect aesthetics, water drainage, and other measurement areas that were judged satisfactory by the preliminary analysis made before the reduction in open space. A second quick look at all measures after ameliorative changes are suggested might help guard against such problems.

5. *Groups of impacts may have synergistic effects; groups of minor impacts may produce major ones.*

Examples of negative synergistic effects are changes in noise levels, air quality, and sidewalk width that, taken alone, would not reduce informal recreational use of sidewalks, but together create an intolerably unpleasant environment for that use. This implies that measures should be considered not just one by one relative to their own standards, but also in groups to identify the combined effects. One of the benefits found by Phoenix in using a measurement checklist was the identification of minor impacts that, together, could affect a decision but that might have been overlooked if an ad hoc approach had been used.

6. *The accuracy of quantitative estimates is likely to be unknown or poor for some important impact areas.*

Ranges rather than just single number estimates should be given where possible. Sensitivity analyses should be considered to see how results would change as assumptions vary. (Sensitivity analyses are relatively rare in impact evaluations, though common in business and engineering decisions where exact values of key input variables are uncertain.) The degree of uncertainty in estimates should be stated explicitly, as best as possible, so decision makers and the public know how much to rely on them. It is important to explain when you are guessing and when you have a solid analysis.

7. *Some types of impacts are difficult or inappropriate to quantify; these should be assessed qualitatively, not ignored.*

More impacts can be quantified than is generally realized. Attempts should be made to define and at least approximately quantify all impacts; one should not give up too soon on this. However, where quantification is difficult or inappropriate, or when time or know-how is lacking, qualitative assessments should be made. Strong consensus was reached by our Advisory Group on this point.[3] For example, if a proposed development creates a hazard to neighborhood children by increasing street traffic, it is preferable to note the potential danger than to ignore it because the level of danger cannot be quantitatively

---

3. Based on comments at second Advisory Group meeting, December 11, 1975, at The Urban Institute, Washington, D.C.

expressed. Likewise, if a development appears likely to attract additional related industries, this secondary economic impact should be noted in some form, even if the number of resulting new jobs generated for the community cannot be reasonably estimated.

The danger of losing the perspective of the "big picture" while observing the individual pieces can happen whether a checklist is used or not. Qualitative overviews in narrative form may help guard against this problem.

8. *Consistency and fairness of evaluation can be improved if documented checklists and documented data collection procedures are used.*

This assertion is somewhat at odds with Number 3 above. Use of a checklist would ensure a consistent starting point; presentation of results at least would then indicate explicitly the set of impacts considered and those for which detailed analyses were judged appropriate. But judgments must still be made regarding which impacts on the checklist to analyze in detail. Rules of thumb can be used for initial screenings to see whether in-depth evaluation is needed, but such rules may let some important situations worthy of analysis be overlooked or they may trigger some unnecessary analyses.

9. *Legal, political, and organizational constraints on applying systematic comprehensive measurement procedures can be at least partially overcome.*

If an evaluation methodology can be shown to be fair and reliable—or at least better than if it were not used—its use may be upheld. The participating governments and the Advisory Group to this study strongly support this view.

THE PROPOSED METHOD—AN OVERVIEW

Based on the above assumptions, the approach summarized below is proposed for local government evaluation of proposed land development. Later chapters discuss the approach in more detail, its pros and cons, and how to determine its appropriateness in particular settings. The basic steps in the approach are as follows:

1. Develop a set of impact measures that will reflect effects of development on local community objectives and key citizen concerns. (Chapter III illustrates a set of objectives and measures.) The list may be used internally by the planning staff (as was tried in Indianapolis) or by all concerned with development—citizens, planning staff, and elected officials (as was attempted in Phoenix).

2. Develop initial familiarity with each development to be reviewed and its surroundings, through site visits; developer's plans and analysis; preliminary meetings with citizens, developers, and other interested parties; and background data available on the site and neighborhood.

3. Review, at least briefly, each development for which a rezoning, variance, special exemption, or other government approval is needed, using the entire checklist of measures. The review may use a mixture of rough quantitative and qualitative methods. Even small developments may have significant localized, if not communitywide, effects. Many impact measurements will be irrelevant or trivial, and can be immediately dropped. Others—usually most of the rest—will require only "back-of-the-envelope" or qualitative analysis. Only a few, if any, may require in-depth analysis.

4. Undertake in-depth analyses, where this is possible, of potential impacts that appear likely to be of major significance—at least when the information might affect the decision or if a rigorous analysis might be needed to avert or support court action. Accuracy only to the level needed for decision making is necessary; often quite crude approximations suffice. In many cases, data provided by developers will suffice, assuming that planners check the validity of the data.

5. Compare likely impacts of the proposed development to those that would occur if the development does not proceed. The demand that led to the proposal may have to be satisfied somewhere else in the community either by new development at other locations or by further use or overcrowding of existing public facilities or housing stock. Otherwise, the demand may be frustrated. Likewise, economic benefits may be displaced elsewhere.

6. Consider impacts of the proposal with and without ameliorating changes if there are viable alternatives.

7. Present the results of the analysis, using tables summarizing the findings for each measure (see examples in Chapter VII) and a narrative

highlighting the major tradeoffs. The narrative can also deal with (a) potential chains of events that may be set off by the development (that is, the secondary effects of development) and (b) other impacts not reflected by individual measurements, or not evident from looking at measurements one by one, such as changes in business opportunities, increased reliance on vehicles, images of the community, opportunities for alternative lifestyles, and so forth. This allows special considerations not reflected by the measurement list to be taken into account.

8. Keep track of the cumulative impacts of development—or, more realistically some simple proxies for them—periodically, no less than annually. This is probably done best by analysis outside the process of one-by-one decisions. It helps provide a check on whether comprehensive plans are still adequate. "Targets" can be set for many types of impacts. Running sums kept as developments are proposed can reveal whether targets or tipping points are neared. If so, more detailed analysis of cumulative effects is warranted. The additional number of acres that can be made impervious before flooding becomes a high risk and the additional emissions that can be tolerated before air quality nears undesirable levels are examples of impacts for which targets may be precomputed based on community objectives and current (baseline) conditions. These targets may be included as part of the comprehensive planning process, as is being tried in Montgomery County, Maryland. This tends to shift much of the analysis burden from the review of individual project proposals to the development of community plans. [4]

RELATION TO OTHER APPROACHES

Other evaluation approaches for satisfying the evaluation needs implicit in the assumptions expressed earlier in this chapter, in addition to the recommended checklist approach, can be cited. In the discussion of three approaches here, it should be noted that, especially in practice, the differences may be largely a matter of degree.

Ad Hoc or "Organic" Evaluations[5]

This is the most prevalent form of evaluation today, especially in smaller planning departments. Typically, an individual in a development review group of the planning department, given responsibility to coordinate the evaluation, plays a large role in deciding what to evaluate, the form of the evaluation, and the tools to be used. In important cases, consultants may be hired.

The impact areas to be analyzed are often determined by such factors as: citizen concerns in the vicinity of the proposed development; knowledge of public reactions to similar developments in the past; the available time, tools, and staff for analysis; the data provided by the developer; and local, political or technical "hot" issues of the day. However, many of these same considerations would influence which measures on a checklist were chosen for rough or detailed analyses, so the two approaches, while starting from different points, may follow similar paths.

In some communities where the decision making body has generally approved proposals unless shown reasons not to, the ad hoc staff evaluation emphasis may be primarily on negative attributes. Less frequently, the emphasis may be on advantages of the new development.

The ad hoc approach has much to recommend it. It allows a development to be reviewed from whatever angles seem most appropriate for the case at hand, regardless of whether they are easily cast into "measures." But the flexibility and informality also can lead to inconsistency in treatment from one case to another, and to missing important impacts through failure to give them even cursory attention. And since the approach may continually change in presentation and methodology, it may take longer and be more difficult for decision makers to understand the evaluation presented, especially in respect to getting a sense of the reliability of the data.

There is no reason, however, why the main virtue of the ad hoc approach—its flexibility—can not be combined with the use of a measurement checklist. The checklist approach, while ensuring

---

4. Target-setting is discussed further in Chapter VI and, as it applies to environmental impacts, in D. Keyes, op. cit.

5. The term "organic" reflects the fact that choices for analysis grow out of the situation at hand.

comprehensiveness and some minimum consistency, need not constrain the evaluation.

Preplanned Tools
Used in "Organic" Evaluations

This approach is currently being used by some of the more advanced planning departments. It is characterized by the availability of a repertory of impact analysis tools, possibly including sophisticated computer models and predigested impact analyses built into comprehensive plans which become applicable for a certain time period and a certain geographic area.

Rather than starting from a checklist, the approach selected for a particular evaluation evolves from the case at hand—hence the term "organic." The project review staff exercises ad hoc judgment about which points to consider, which tools to use, and how closely the particular project must fit the predigested analyses built into the comprehensive plan. Some aspects of the evaluation may be administratively defined, such that the project review staff is required to consider certain types of impacts, use certain simulation models, or make a finding with respect to the applicability of the predigested analyses in the plan.

The results of this preplanned tools approach are even more likely than those of the ad hoc approach to resemble the results obtained by starting with an explicit checklist of measures. Again, they are not mutually exclusive. Combining the checklist approach with preplanned tools could have the advantage of standardizing presentations and ensuring that important aspects are not overlooked.

Successive Screening Approach

Another approach, basically similar to the approach recommended in this report, has been developed by Planning Environment International, a division of Alan M. Vorhees and Associates, Inc. for HUD.[6] Although initially aimed at evaluation of HUD-sponsored projects as required by the National Environmental Policy Act of 1969 and HUD's own guidelines, the methodology has broader application to many types of development reviews.

_____
6. *Interim Guide for Environmental Assessment,* op. cit.

The basic concept is a two-part review: first, an initial screening, then, "higher level tests." The initial screening involves about 79 environmental "components" including subsidence, soil permeability, ground water flow direction, diversity of biota, transportation, noise, crowding, and visual content. The standards used in the screening range from legally mandated federal standards, as in the case for air and water, to commonly used rules of thumb, such as specified acres of recreation space per capita.

Only those projects which have components which are "of question" or which "appear unacceptable" require in-depth testing using "higher level tests." These higher tests actually involve a hierarchy of tests of increasing complexity, with only a very few components, ordinarily earmarked for the most detailed tests—similar to the application of the evaluation approach presented in this report.

The Vorhees study and our own are complementary in many ways. Both are fundamentally concerned with achieving clearer and more comprehensive evaluations, stressing practical techniques and quantified impacts insofar as possible. The following comparisons may be helpful to readers of both reports:

- The Vorhees study emphasizes the suitability of site conditions for proposed projects, but also includes impacts on the community. Our Urban Institute study emphasizes the impact of the projects on the community.

- The Vorhees study covers a broader range of environmental impacts than does the Institute study, but does not include economic impacts, as does the Institute study.

- The Vorhees study describes what is needed for the higher tests in terms of agencies involved, types of experts, and data requirements; it does not dwell in detail on the analysis procedures for the tests. The Institute study assesses alternative computer models and other evaluation techniques, explaining them in considerable detail.

- The Vorhees study emphasizes initial screening against predetermined standards or rules of thumb, using as measures some end results but also some intermediate factors. The Institute study emphasizes end impacts on people and the measures for assessing those impacts, but it leaves the setting of standards to the local governments. (Because the Vorhees study was designed originally to assist in evaluations by HUD field offices, its approach was developed to assure consistency from place to place.)

It is probably evident from these comparisons that local and higher level jurisdictions that are developing evaluation programs could profit by giving consideration to both studies.

III. SUGGESTED MEASURES

Local concerns and conditions vary too much for exactly the same set of impact measures to meet the needs of all local governments. The microclimate is a frequent concern in San Francisco where skyscrapers can generate annoying wind currents at street level; this is rarely a problem in Washington, D.C., where building heights are severely restricted. Coyote calls and desert life are vital issues in Phoenix, where proximity to nature is viewed as a major asset; the wildlife concerns of Pittsburgh or Boston are quite different.

Although one set of measures may not be appropriate everywhere, there *is* much commonality in the set of impacts that are of concern to citizens generally. Much of the variation from place to place relates to how *frequently* a particular issue occurs rather than to whether it *ever* is of importance.

This chapter presents a set of impact measures that seeks to address the most widespread concerns. It illustrates the types of measures that might be used as a starting point for governments wishing to create their own lists. First, some considerations in the selection of impact measures are given. Organizational aspects of implementing a measurement system are discussed in Chapter VIII.

CHOOSING A SET OF MEASURES

To develop a set of measures most applicable to local concerns, it is useful to proceed in three steps: (1) identify community objectives and the associated types of impacts of most importance locally, now and in the foreseeable future, (2) de-fine specific measures for each impact area, and (3) identify data collection and the best available analysis procedures for each measure.

Variations on a basic set of measures may be needed for different types of land use changes (residential and industrial) different administrative or legal frameworks (rezoning, variance, and special exceptions), or for different stages in decision making (plan formulation, individual development review by planning staff, planning commission review, and appeals). However, governments should consider developing one master list of impact areas and associated measures to encourage as much consistency and similarity of approach for the different applications as possible.

Identifying Types of Impacts To Be Measured

Each of the communitywide or neighborhood conditions considered important and likely to be impacted by development should be a candidate for measurement. At the most general level, virtually all communities will be concerned with development impacts on the local economy, natural environment, public services, certain private services, and on social, aesthetic, and cultural conditions.[1] More specific impact areas of local concern can be identified from:

---

1. Health and safety conditions for potential users of new development, also of prime concern, are usually guarded today by health, building, and fire codes. The aspects of citizen health and safety usually protected by such codes do not require additional impact measures, but rather a determination of whether the codes are met.

- *Statements of community objectives and goals.* This might be something like the hypothetical set in Exhibit 2, or the extensive "Goals for Dallas,"[2] or the comprehensive and detailed Indianapolis goals statements. The latter, though not officially adopted, are noteworthy for their concept and level of detail.

- *Federal, state, and local legislation.* This includes, for example, the enabling legislation for planning, zoning, and noise ordinances, and/or for community appearance commissions. The legislation should be reviewed to identify impact areas that *must* be considered and to identify community goals and objectives (sometimes alluded to or included in the legislation). Some types of impacts, such as aesthetics, are required to be considered in some communities while they are constrained or disallowed by the courts in others.

- *Analysis of past local development reviews, hearings, and development-related court cases.* For example, Exhibit 1, Chapter II, shows the issues that appeared in newspaper articles about land development cases in three cities over a several-month period. A local government could do a similar but more rigorous tabulation.

- *Recent citizen surveys with questions pertinent to development.* Of special interest are questions identifying levels of citizen dissatisfaction with their community and neighborhoods, reasons for dissatisfaction, and features or aspects of community life considered important and worth preserving.

- *Expressions by citizen groups, private industry, academic leaders, and members of the local government itself.*

These are especially important for identifying issues that may not emerge from the other sources.

Criteria for Choosing Specific Measures

Many rough checklists stop short, listing just the goals to be considered but leaving the details unspecified. This opens the way for much of the vagueness, inconsistency, and hard-to-understand data prevalent today. Thus, once the general qualities have been identified, such as recreational opportunity or employment, specific measures for assessing them should be defined.

To the extent feasible, the measures should have the following attributes:

- *Focus on end impacts.* Citizen concerns, rather than intermediate factors, should be measured. For example, it seems preferable in the field of recreation to determine the number and percent of citizens within x miles of a park and citizens' satisfaction with recreational opportunities, rather than the number of park acres per person. A large number of acres to which residents have poor access and which they dislike when they get there could show up, in the latter type of measure, as superior to a smaller, better distributed, higher quality system. Similarly, it seems preferable to emphasize changes in tolerable uses (e.g., prohibited for drinking, swimming, or boating) of nearby water bodies, rather than the amount of new effluents that will run into them, since the latter fails to show, except to a few pollution specialists, what the public effect will be. Again, changes in travel times or average travel speeds convey more clearly to most motorists what the congestion effects will be than would changes in the number of vehicles per hour.

- *Be readily understandable and interpretable.* Technical jargon should be avoided or at least defined. Converting sets of variables into weighted indexes

2. Southwest Center for Advanced Studies, *Proposals for Achieving the Goals for Dallas,* Dallas, Texas, 1969.

EXHIBIT 2

COMMUNITY OBJECTIVES FOR REGULATING LAND DEVELOPMENT[1]

I. Local Economy:

To keep the local government fiscally solvent without excessive taxes; to maintain a high level of stable employment and to reduce unemployment and under-employment in the community; to maintain prosperity; and to enable citizens in the community to achieve levels of personal income and wealth consistent with a decent standard of living.

II. Natural Environment:

To minimize pollution, protect wildlife and ecologically important features, preserve the natural environment, and conserve scarce resources.

III. Aesthetic and Cultural Values:

To protect and improve the physical and cultural attractiveness of the community.

IV. Public and Private Services:

- *Health and Safety.* To minimize illness, injury, premature death rates, and property loss or damage.
- *Recreation.* To provide a variety of accessible and enjoyable recreational facilities and programs in the community.
- *Education.* To provide quality education at all levels for all people in the community; to provide as diverse educational experiences as the community requires; and to assure the convenience and pleasantness of attending school.
- *Local Transportation.* To provide access to an adequate choice of community services, facilities, and employment in a safe, quick, and convenient manner; and to move goods efficiently.
- *Shopping.* To promote the adequacy, variety, convenience and pleasantness of shopping for people in the community.

V. Housing and Social Conditions

- *Housing.* To increase the opportunity for all citizens to obtain satisfactory housing at prices they can afford.
- *Social Concerns and Community Morale.* To promote friendliness, psychological well-being, and good community morale while protecting individuals' privacy and ability to regulate their interpersonal contacts.
- *Fairness to All Groups.* To apply each objective with equity to all within the community.

---

1. This set of objectives is illustrative. Each community should determine goals consistent with the desires and values of its citizens. The order of the objectives implies no ranking of priorities.

is undesirable because the process tends to hide the assumptions, tradeoffs, and value judgments behind the weightings.

- *Data collection procedures should be practical, reasonably reliable, and affordable.* Some desirable measures can not be used for lack of adequate ways to estimate them. For example, many people are concerned that a development will make their neighborhood feel more crowded and less friendly, but there seems to be no satisfactory or reliable way to estimate such effects at present.

  To be practical, the data needed for each measure must be available at the decision time. Measures dealing with perceived attractiveness, for example, cannot be used for many rezoning decisions because the details of site design often are not ready to subject to analysis far enough in advance of the decision. Thus only gross aesthetic considerations such as the scale of highrise buildings relative to surrounding neighborhoods are feasible in those situations. For Planned Unit Developments (PUDs), however, as well as for other cases, the needed data often are available. Different variations of a measure may be needed for the different decision points.

- *Satisfy existing legal requirements and constraints.* Having some measures related to noise and aesthetics, for example, may not be sufficient. Laws and ordinances often mandate the specific measures to be used, such as the maximum noise levels allowable for certain zoning classes, or the percent of a site that must be landscaped. Measures must be consistent with these limits. Some laws or court decisions imply that certain measures cannot be used in making the land use decision—or at least cannot be the major reason for preventing a development. Aesthetics is an example of a consideration disallowed in some communities.

- *Avoid repetition.* The set of measures should contain a minimum of redundancy, even though the various measurement areas are interrelated. Some redundancy may be desirable, however, to allow checks on information reliability.

Admittedly, there are many considerations to worry about. But local governments should not give up too quickly when trying to identify appropriate measures for a community concern, especially for "soft," difficult to quantify impacts. Often reasonable surrogates can be found, if direct measures are not available.

ILLUSTRATIVE CHECKLIST OF MEASURES

For communities interested in developing their own set of measures, the illustrative set shown in Exhibit 3 might be used as a starting point. The impact areas in Exhibit 3 conform to the hypothetical statement of objectives in Exhibit 2. The associated measures were selected with an eye to the criteria listed above.[3]

The grouping and ordering of measures under the subject headings in Exhibit 3 are discretionary; other groups could also be used. The set is not intended to be used in a particular sequence. It matters little whether an impact such as noise pollution is listed under "natural environment" or as a "social" impact so long as it is considered for its impact on pleasantness of environment. And regardless of the categories in which they are listed, their interrelationships need to be taken into account.

Some groupings of measures which cut across the categories used in Exhibit 3 are of special interest. The set of measures relating to citizen perceptions of various neighborhood conditions (air quality, attractiveness, service availability, sociability, etc.) should be considered as a group, as well as one-by-one, to see the overall pattern and to identify the relatively worst problem areas.[4]

---

3. Exhibit 3 uses the same headings and presents measures in the same order as in the initial report in this series (Schaenman and Muller, op. cit.). They are quite similar overall and in intent, in spite of a few changes, additions, and deletions. The final column in Exhibit 3—"References"—provides a key for getting from the specific measures to other reports in this series which discuss them in greater detail.

4. The use and perceptions of neighborhood impacts are discussed further in Christensen, op. cit.

EXHIBIT 3

SUGGESTED IMPACT MEASURES

IMPACT AREA AND SUBAREAS		USUALLY APPLICABLE TO EVALUATING[1]			BASES FOR ESTIMATES[2]	REF-ER-ENCES[3]
Preferred Measures	Fallback Measures	Comprehensive Plans, Cumulative Effects, Large Rezonings	Small to Medium Residential Rezoning	Small to Medium Commercial-Industrial Rezoning		
I. *Local Economy*						
Public Fiscal Balance						
1. Net change in government fiscal flow (revenues less expenditures).		x			*Public revenues:* expected household incomes by residential housing type; added property values. *Public expenditures:* analysis of new service demand; current costs; available capacities by service.	M
Employment						
2. Change in numbers and percent employed, unemployed, underemployed, by skill level.	2a. Number of net new long-term and short-term jobs provided to local area.	x		x	Direct from new business; or estimated from floor space, local residential patterns, expected immigration, current unemployment profiles.	
Wealth						
3. Change in land values.		x	x	x	Supply and demand of similarly zoned land, environmental changes near property.	
II. *Natural Environment*						
Air Quality						
Health						
4. Change in air pollution concentrations by frequency of occurrence and number of people at risk.[4]	4a. Change in air pollutant concentrations relative to standards.	x		x	Current ambient concentrations, current and expected emissions, dispersion models, population maps.	K
	4b. Change in pollutant emissions relative to emission "budgets"[5] or targets.					
Nuisance						
5. Change in occurrence of visual (smoke, haze) or olfactory (odor) air quality nuisances, and number of people affected.[6]	5a. Changes in the likelihood that air quality nuisances (qualitative judgment) will occur or vary in severity.	x		x	Baseline citizen survey, expected industrial processes, traffic volumes.	K,C
Water Quality						
6. Changes in permissible or tolerable water uses and number of people affected—for each relevant body of water.	6a. Change in water pollutant concentrations (relative to standards), for each water pollutant.	x		x	Current and expected effluents, current ambient concentrations, water quality model.	K
	6b. Change in amount discharged into body of water relative to effluent "budgets" for each pollutant.[5]					
Noise						
7. Change in noise levels and frequency of occurrence, and number of people bothered.[6]	7a. Changes in traffic levels, sound barriers, and other factors likely to affect noise levels and perceived satisfaction.	x	x	x	Changes in nearby traffic or other noise sources, and in noise barriers; noise propagation model or nomographs relating noise levels to traffic, barriers, etc.; baseline citizen survey of current satisfaction with noise levels.	K,C

EXHIBIT 3 (CONT.)

SUGGESTED IMPACT MEASURES

IMPACT AREA AND SUBAREAS		USUALLY APPLICABLE TO EVALUATING[1]			BASES FOR ESTIMATES[2]	REF-ER-ENCES[3]
Preferred Measures	Fallback Measures	Comprehensive Plans, Cumulative Effects, Large Rezonings	Small to Medium			
			Residential Rezoning	Commercial-Industrial Rezoning		
Wildlife and Vegetation						
8. Change in diversity and population size (abundance) of wildlife and vegetation (including trees) of common species.[7]	8a. Changes in amount and quality of (a) habitat by animal type; (b) green space, or (c) number of mature trees.	x	x	x	Wildlife and vegetation inventory; expected removal of cover or changes to habitats.	K
9. Change in numbers of rare or endangered species.	9a. Same as 8a.	x	x	x	Same as 8a.	K
Natural Disasters						
10. Change in number of people and value of property endangered by: flooding, earthquakes, landslides, mudslides, and other natural disasters, by frequency of occurrence.	10a. Change in flooding frequency. 10b. Change in percent of land with impermeable cover relative to "budgeted" levels.[8]	x	x	x	Flood plain and other hazard maps; changes in local topography and sewering; change in percent permeable cover; stream flow and hydraulic models.	K
III. Aesthetics and Cultural Values						
Attractiveness						
11. Change in number and percent of citizens who are satisfied with neighborhood appearance.	11a. Disturbance of physical conditions currently considered attractive; removal/improvement of conditions currently rated unattractive.	x	x	x	Baseline citizen survey of ratings of current attractiveness and identification of problems and assets; visual simulation of proposed development using retouched photos, drawings or 3-D models for assessing future preferences using a sample of citizens.	C
View Opportunities						
12. Change in number or percent of citizens satisfied with views from their homes (or businesses).	12a. Number of households (or businesses) whose views are blocked, degraded, or improved.	x	x	x	Baseline citizen survey; geometric analysis of structures to identify view opportunities before and after development.	C
Landmarks						
13. Number and perceived importance of cultural, historic, or scientific landmarks to be lost, made less accessible, or made more accessible.	13a. Rarity of landmark and distance to nearest similar examples of landmarks to be lost (or made more accessible).	x	x	x	Inventory and importance ranking of landmarks; survey of citizens and scholars regarding importance.	C
IV. Public and Private Services						
Drinking Water						
Availability						
14. Change in frequency duration and severity of water shortage incidents, and number of people affected.	14a. Change in likelihood of increased water shortages, and number of people likely to be affected.	x		x	Current usage, expected new demand; projected supplies.	K
Quality						
15. Change in salinity and other indices of drinking water quality and safety, and number of people affected.[9]	15a. Changes in effluents or purification processing likely to affect taste or other qualities of drinking water.	x	x	x	Expected effluents from new development; purification process used; current and expected usage; profile of underground water system.	K

EXHIBIT 3 (CONT.)
SUGGESTED IMPACT MEASURES

IMPACT AREA AND SUBAREAS		USUALLY APPLICABLE TO EVALUATING[1]			BASES FOR ESTIMATES[2]	REF-ER-ENCES[3]
Preferred Measures	Fallback Measures	Comprehensive Plans, Cumulative Effects, Large Rezonings	Small to Medium			
			Residential Rezoning	Commercial-Industrial Rezoning		
Hospital Care						
Emergency Care Availability						
16. Change in number of citizens beyond x minutes travel time from emergency health care.		x	x	x	Maps of population distribution and emergency facilities; number of emergency vehicles (if any), expected calls, and dispatch policy.	
Availability/Crowdedness						
17. Change in potential bed need versus bed supply of area hospitals, by type of clinical service (medical, surgical, pediatric, obstetrical).		x	x		Current patient hospital bed days per 1000 population by sex-age group and medical service; available bed capacities; expected population by sex-age group.	
Crime Control						
Crime Rate						
18. Change in rate of crimes in existing community.	18a. Expert rating of change in crime hazard.	x	x	x	Current crime rates and case histories of similar neighborhood changes; changes in community lighting, sightlines, hiding places, people mix.	
Feeling of Security						
19. Change in percent of people feeling a lack of security from crime.	19a. Change in people mix, police patrolling, and physical conditions (lighting, sightlines, potential hiding places, etc.) likely to affect feelings of security.	x	x	x	Baseline citizen survey plus the data above.	C
Fire Protection						
20. Change in fire incidence, property loss, and casualty rates.	20a. Expert ratings of change in likelihood of fires, fire spread, rescue hazards.	x	x	x	Incidence rates by occupancy types; people mix; available water supply; available fire suppression equipment and manning; likely building materials; site plan if available.	
Recreation–Public Facilities[10]						
Overall Satisfaction						
21. Change in number and percent of households satisfied with public recreation opportunities.	21a. Measure 23 (change in accessibility) and changes in other physical conditions (noise, air quality, hazards, crowdedness) likely to affect satisfaction, and number of households potentially affected.	x	x	x	Baseline citizen surveys, and expected changes in facilities and environment (noise, air quality, dangers).	C
22. Change in number or percent of households using facilities (viewed relative to nominal capacity), by facility.[11]	22a. Same as above.	x	x	x	Citizen survey.	C

EXHIBIT 3 (CONT.)
SUGGESTED IMPACT MEASURES

IMPACT AREA AND SUBAREAS		USUALLY APPLICABLE TO EVALUATING[1]			BASES FOR ESTIMATES[2]	REF-ER-ENCES[3]
Preferred Measures	Fallback Measures	Comprehensive Plans, Cumulative Effects, Large Rezonings	Small to Medium			
			Residential Rezoning	Commercial-Industrial Rezoning		
Accessibility						
23. Change in number and percent of households with access to various types of recreation facilities within x minutes travel, by type of facility and mode of travel.[11]		x	x	x	Maps of facilities and distribution of population; citizen survey of travel mode.	C
Recreation—Informal Settings *Overall Satisfaction*						
24. Change in number or percent of households satisfied with recreation in informal outdoor spaces in neighborhood.	24a. Measure 25 (availability) and change in other physical condition likely to affect satisfaction and number of households potentially affected.	x	x		Baseline citizen survey and observation of current usage patterns; physical environment changes expected.	C
Availability						
25. Change in availability of informal physical settings for recreation and number of people affected.			x		Changes in open space and physical environment expected.	C
Education *Accessibility/Convenience*						
26. Change in number and percent of households satisfied with accessibility of schools.	26a. Change in location of schools, and physical conditions around schools or along routes to schools that are likely to affect satisfaction with accessibility.	x	x		Citizen survey; changes in available path, nearby traffic conditions en route to schools.	C
27. Change in number and percent of students within x minutes, by type of school and travel mode.		x	x		Map of school and population distribution; busing records.	C
28. Number and percent of students having to switch schools or busing status.		x	x		Relation of capacity to expected demands, and school board policy.	
Crowdedness						
29. Change in school crowdedness indicators; e.g., student-teacher ratios, number of shifts.		x	x		Citizen survey; expected change in noise, traffic hazard, air quality, other hazards.	
Transportation—Mass Transit *Satisfaction*						
30. Change in number and percent of households satisfied with mass transit service.	30a. Expected changes in scheduling, routing, or crowdedness, and number of households likely to be affected.	x			Citizen survey, expected service changes, expected change in factors affecting satisfaction.	C

EXHIBIT 3 (CONT.)
SUGGESTED IMPACT MEASURES

IMPACT AREA AND SUBAREAS		USUALLY APPLICABLE TO EVALUATING[1]			BASES FOR ESTIMATES[2]	REF-ER-ENCES[3]
Preferred Measures	Fallback Measures	Comprehensive Plans, Cumulative Effects, Large Rezonings	Small to Medium			
			Residential Rezoning	Commercial-Industrial Rezoning		
	30b. For retrospective studies: changes in number and percent of (a) households and (b) trips using public transit.	x			Usage levels, from fares and surveys.	C
Accessibility						
31. Change in number and percent of citizens residing (or working) within x feet of public transit stop.		x	x	x		C
Transportation—Pedestrians						
Satisfaction/Accessibility						
32. Change in number and percent of households satisfied with walking conditions and walking opportunities in their neighborhood.[12]	32a. Change in physical conditions (sidewalks, noise, etc.) affecting current satisfaction or dissatisfaction with walking conditions, and number of households likely to be affected.	x	x	x	Baseline citizen survey, estimated changes in physical walking conditions; additions or removals of desired destinations.	C
Safety						
See measures 33 and 34 below.	32b. The group of measures of accessibility to shopping, schools (27), recreation (23), public transit (31).	x	x	x	N/A	
Transportation—Private Vehicles						
Safety						
33. Change in number and percent of households satisfied with traffic safety (vehicle and pedestrian).	33a. Change in physical conditions (e.g., traffic volumes, sidewalk width, barriers from traffic) likely to affect perceived safety, and number of households likely to be affected.	x	x	x	Baseline citizen survey, changes in traffic and traffic controls; circulation patterns.	C
34. Change in number and severity of accidents per 1,000 persons by pedestrians and riders.	34a. Change in number and severity of traffic hazards created (may include changes in traffic volume and speed, sightlines, traffic controls), and number of people potentially affected.	x	x	x	Accident frequency and causation data; changes in traffic and traffic controls, circulation patterns, expected traffic volumes.	
Travel Time						
35. Change in vehicular travel times between selected origins and destinations, by time of day and day of week.	35a. Change in "level of service" for selected roads and intersections, by time of day.[13]	x		x	Current traffic volumes; changes in street layout, width and traffic controls; estimated net new vehicle trips.	

EXHIBIT 3 (CONT.)
SUGGESTED IMPACT MEASURES

IMPACT AREA AND SUBAREAS		USUALLY APPLICABLE TO EVALUATING[1]			BASES FOR ESTIMATES[2]	REF-ER-ENCES[3]
Preferred Measures	Fallback Measures	Comprehensive Plans, Cumulative Effects, Large Rezonings	Small to Medium			
			Residential Rezoning	Commercial-Industrial Rezoning		
Parking Availability						
36. Change in average time needed to find acceptable parking space within x feet of residence (or desired destinations) in neighborhood of development, by time of day and day of week.	36a. Change in the ratio of demand for parking spaces to supply of spaces within x distance of destinations in neighborhood of development, by type of space (metered, all-day, sheltered, etc.)	x	x	x	Current spaces available; new demand and supply; math model for estimating parking times (not needed for 36a).	
37. Percent of drivers finding neighborhood parking satisfactory.	37a. Same as 36a.	x	x	x	Baseline citizen survey; expected changes in supply and demand for spaces.	C
Shopping[14]						
38. Change in number and percent of households satisfied with shopping opportunities.	38a. Change in variety, accessibility, and physical conditions of shopping areas.	x		x	Baseline citizen survey; change in physical conditions around shopping areas.	C
39. Change in number and percent of households within x minutes travel time to shopping, by type store and mode of travel.		x		x	Map showing location of stores and population, before and after development.	C
Energy Services						
40. Change in the frequency and duration of energy shortages, and the number of people affected, by fuel type.	40a. Expected energy usage per unit area of floor space or per unit of production, relative to standards for usage, by type of buildings and land use.	x	x[15]	x	Current and expected usage and supply in community; design and construction of buildings; type of manufacturing activity expected.	
Housing						
41. Change in number and percent of housing units that are substandard and the number of people living in them.		x	x	x	Current housing stock conditions, number to be removed or improved.	
42. Change in number and percent of housing units relative to need, by type of housing (price, owner/rental, number of bedrooms, style, etc.).	42a. Change in number of units by type, viewed relative to number of families in various income groups in the community.	x	x	x	Current profile of housing stock units added or destroyed; past housing chain effects in distribution of population by income level, indicators of latent demand for housing.	
V. **Other Social Impacts** *(in addition to those included above)*[16]						
People Displacement						
43. Number of residents (or workers) displaced by development, and whether satisfied with move.	43a. Number of persons displaced.	x	x	x	Number of persons living in building to be destroyed; special survey of them.	C
Special Hazards						
44. Number of children physically at risk from "special" hazards created by development (e.g., machinery, junk, unguarded deep water).			x	x	Physical outdoor changes expected.	C

EXHIBIT 3 (CONT.)
SUGGESTED IMPACT MEASURES

IMPACT AREA AND SUBAREAS		USUALLY APPLICABLE TO EVALUATING[1]	Small to Medium		BASES FOR ESTIMATES[2]	REF-ER-ENCES[3]
Preferred Measures	Fallback Measures	Comprehensive Plans, Cumulative Effects, Large Rezonings	Residential Rezoning	Commercial-Industrial Rezoning		
Sociability/Friendliness[17]						
45. Change in social interaction patterns (e.g., frequency of neighboring, community activities).	45a. Identification of changes in people mix, settings for social activities, and physical barriers to social interactions.	x	x	x	Baseline survey of current neighboring and community activity patterns; changes in availability of community and small group meeting places; changes in physical barriers (e.g., highways, fences, heavy traffic, buildings which hinder access from one area of a neighborhood to another or footbridges or removal of barriers linking the areas); changes in people mix.	C
Privacy						
46. Change in number and percent of households satisfied with privacy in outdoor areas around home.	46a. Change in sightlines, pedestrian volumes, or other conditions likely to affect satisfaction, and number of households potentially affected.	x	x	x	Citizen survey; geometric analysis of sightlines; changes in sight and sound barriers.	C
Overall Contentment with Neighborhood						
47. Change in number and percent of citizens satisfied with their residential (or work) neighborhood.	47a. Degree of change to neighborhood elements that citizens express most satisfaction or dissatisfaction with.	x	x	x	Citizen survey using data from other measures.	C

NOTES:

1. Most measures are directly applicable at one time or another to all types of development.

2. The "bases for estimate" column presents a simplified, brief listing of key data and models (if any) needed for the preferred measure. A subset of the data is needed for the backup measures unless otherwise indicated. For retrospective studies, other, more direct measurement procedures are often feasible. Data collection procedures for the measures are outlined in P.S. Schaenman and T. Muller, *Measuring Impacts of Land Development,* Washington, D.C., The Urban Institute, 1974. A more detailed discussion of data collection and analysis may be found in the references.

3. Reference codes:

M = Muller, *Fiscal Impacts of Land Development: A Critique of Methods and Review of Issues,* The Urban Institute, Washington, D.C., 1975.

C = Christensen, *Social Impacts of Land Development: An Initial Approach for Estimating Impacts on Neighborhood Usages and Perceptions,* The Urban Institute, Washington, D.C., 1976.

K = Keyes, *Land Development and the Natural Environment: Estimating Impacts,* The Urban Institute, Washington, D.C., 1976.

4. Measure 4 could be expanded, where appropriate, to reflect damage to vegetation and materials as well as to people's health.

EXHIBIT 3 (CONT.)
SUGGESTED IMPACT MEASURES

NOTES: *(Cont.)*

5. "Emission budgets" would be maximum amounts of additional pollutants that could be added in a year. They would be based on desirable or tolerable ambient concentrations of each pollutant. The "budgets" should be revised periodically as part of comprehensive planning.

6. Citizen satisfaction with air quality and noise levels is "built into" Measures 5 and 7, respectively, via local calibration of what constitutes annoying levels for people to be affected. However, for retrospective studies, a separate measure of "percent of citizens satisfied with neighborhood air quality (or noise) levels" might also be desirable.

7. Diversity is measured by the number of species present or by "diversity index scores"—see Keyes, op. cit.

8. Similar to the emission budgets (see note 5), a budget for the net additional amount of land that can have impermeable ground cover before flooding becomes a likely hazard that can specified based on the relation between impermeable cover, stormwater runoff, stream flow, and flood levels for individual watersheds.

9. Measure 6 is complementary to Measure 15; it reflects changes in quality of bodies of water from which drinking water is drawn, which may or may not affect water quality at the tap.

10. The recreation measures are worded for residential development, but can be restated for commercial/industrial development to indicate the number or percent of affected employees or shoppers; e.g., to estimate the availability and pleasantness of parks for lunch-time use.

11. Measures 22 (usage) and 23 (accessibility) are in part proxies for Measure 21 (satisfaction). But because citizen expectations affect satisfaction so much, the more "objective" measures are also important to consider, especially when there is considerable population turnover.

12. This measure of pedestrian satisfaction is related to other measures which may reflect walking conditions—measures of traffic safety (33,34), air quality (4,5), noise (7), aesthetics (11-13), and measures of accessibility of services (23,27,31). It also reflects changes in the availability of sidewalks, traffic lights, pedestrian bridges, crowdedness of streets, etc., and accessibility of destinations not listed in other measures, such as houses of friends. Satisfaction with walking opportunities might also be reflected by a measure of "changes in amount of walking activity" (number of people walking to destinations in neighborhood at least x times per week).

13. The six "levels of service" are: free flow traffic, stable flow in the upper speed range, stable flow, approaching unstable flow, unstable flow, and forced flow. Each category allows a range of traffic speeds and thus travel times, and describes congestion of the road or intersection. Definitions for each level are given in: *Highway Capacity Manual*, Special Report 87, Highway Research Board, Washington, D.C., 1965.

14. An additional measure, "number and percent of households using existing stores, by type of store," is needed as a baseline for prediction, and may be useful in its own right for retrospective studies.

15. Although individual developments are unlikely to cause noticeable shortages, energy consumption relative to the type of land use—that is, expected efficiency of energy usage—may be maintained on an on-going basis.

16. Because of likely synergistic effects in assessing social impacts on a neighborhood, it seems important to view neighborhood perceptions, service opportunities, and environmental changes together. This cross-cut view of the measures (all those with a "C" in the reference column) is elaborated in Christensen, op. cit.

17. The "change in the percent of citizens perceiving their neighborhood as friendly (or cohesive)" might also be considered for retrospective studies, but seems difficult to forecast with current knowledge. We have not identified a satisfactory proxy for it, and therefore do not include it. Eventually, as data from before-and-after studies are accumulated (or reliable social models are developed), it may be possible to use this measure of a community attribute important to many people.

General note: For brevity, some fallback measures are included in the exhibit to summarize points raised in the detailed reports, even though they are not designated as measures in those reports.

All measures related to accessibility of services (education, recreation, shopping, etc.) form another set of interest—they reveal the extent to which a neighborhood will be dependent on automobiles. Other measurement groupings may be used to define "character of the community" or other concepts used in local evaluations.

Exhibit 4 lists additional measures that seem of less widespread interest, or too difficult to estimate in routine practice, or which do not meet some other criterion, but still may be of interest in some communities now or later as techniques develop.

Preferred and Fallback Position Measures

The measures listed as "preferred" in Exhibit 3 clearly indicate impacts in terms that concern citizens and that are easily interpreted by decision makers. The "fallback" measures represent compromises with the selection criteria, to be used when estimations of the preferred measures are too expensive, not feasible, or of questionable validity. In some cases the fallback measures are intermediate results needed to estimate the preferred measures. In others, they are proxies for the preferred measures. When the connection between the proxy and preferred measures is strong, it may be wasteful to compute the latter. As the state of the art improves, more of the preferred measures will be directly estimatable. Some of the preferred measures that are not yet usable for evaluating proposals can be used today in before-and-after studies, since it is generally more feasible to measure impacts directly than to predict them.

For many types of impacts, it can be argued whether subjective citizen perceptions or objectively measureable changes should be the preferred measures.[5] For example, in assessing recreational opportunities are measures of citizen satisfaction or physical measures of accessibility and variety (such as the percent of citizens within x miles of facilities of specified types) more useful to planners and administrators? We suggest that, where possible, it is desirable to use *both* objective and subjective measures. Citizen perception measures are needed to determine if the physical and social environment is satisfactory in the eyes of the users, not just those of the analyst or decision maker. One cannot assume that by meeting various rules of thumb such as acres of parks per person that local needs will be satisfied. At the same time, physical measures are needed to aid in diagnosis of problems and to indicate whether changes in citizen satisfaction are due to changes in the environment, differences in expectations, or other changes from one group of citizens to another.

Physical measures also are needed because future citizen perceptions are difficult to predict reliably for proposed development, and it is often necessary to measure physical changes and make judgments on the number of people likely to be affected and the magnitude of the impact.[6] For example, the accuracy of predicting how much people's sense of privacy will be affected by new sightlines into their backyards from new, nearby tall buildings is unknown. The best one can probably do is to make the judgment that most people will be adversely affected to some degree if the newly introduced sightlines are the first disturbance to their visual privacy, and then estimate the number of people potentially affected. If they already have little privacy from existing nearby buildings, the addition of another will probably have less impact. As we gain knowledge, perhaps by making more use of before-and-after studies, direct predictions of changes in satisfaction in different situations may become possible.

Localized Versus Areawide Impacts

Many of the measures can be used to express impacts at various scales—block, neighborhood, community, and region. This does not imply that the same data collection and analysis methods are appropriate in each case. For example, a random sample of households might be interviewed to obtain baseline data on current usage of neighborhood facilities, whereas every household on the block in which the development is to occur might

---

5. This is a separate issue from whether citizen perceptions are collected in a scientific way or not—such as citizen surveys based on carefully drawn random samples versus citizen testimony at hearings.

6. Actually, the reliability of estimating how citizens will perceive their neighborhoods after development occurs remains to be established. Because descriptions of potential land development are themselves vague, estimates are on shaky ground.

EXHIBIT 4
SOME OTHER IMPACT MEASURES WORTHY OF CONSIDERATION BUT
NOT INCLUDED ON MAIN LIST

IMPACT AREA	MEASURE	REASON FOR OMISSION FROM MAIN LIST
Local Economy	1. Degree of financial stability of developer.	Hard to measure without access to confidential data. Not universally accepted as business of government. Is an intermediate measure; fiscal, social, aesthetic implications of bankruptcy can be considered as part of other measures.
	2. Change in personal income per household.	Too difficult to estimate, even in the aggregate; too many factors other than new development affect income.
Natural Environment	3. Change in monetary value of pollution-caused damage to health, materials, and vegetation.	Lack of suitable methodology for routine use.
	4. Change in available acres of agricultural or commercial forest land.	Seems more appropriate at regional, state, and national levels, except where a central factor in economy of local jurisdiction.
	5. Change in microclimate (e.g., winds around highrises).	Of interest to only a small fraction of municipalities (e.g., San Francisco) and within them only certain areas. Microclimatic effects on pollution levels are already reflected in Exhibit 3 air pollution measures.
	6. Change in citizen satisfaction with abundance of wild life near home.	Seems difficult to forecast and not meriting effort to try in most communities, in addition to the other wildlife and aesthetics measures already suggested in Exhibit 3.
Aesthetics and Cultural Values	7. Change in community's "image" and "sense of place."	Partially reflected by landmarks and attractiveness measures; difficult to measure what is left over, at least on a routine basis. Not well defined. Not clear whether "increases" in these qualities are desirable.
Public and Private Services	8. Change in storm drainage quality.	Drainage related to major flooding is already reflected in Measure 10, Exhibit 3. Localized flooding should usually be taken care of as part of compliance with building and subdivision codes; however, this might need explicit attention in some situations.
	9. Changes in quality of local government services other than those in Exhibit 3; e.g., solid waste collection and street cleanliness.	Services most likely to be affected by development per se are included in main list. In some cases, additional service measures may be appropriate; e.g., if population density will increase and sanitation department budget is fixed, street cleanliness might be impaired.

EXHIBIT 4 (CONT.)
SOME OTHER IMPACT MEASURES WORTHY OF CONSIDERATION NOT INCLUDED ON MAIN LIST

IMPACT AREA	MEASURE	REASON FOR OMISSION FROM MAIN LIST
Other Social Impacts	10. Change in waiting times for elective surgery in hospitals.	Not a problem in most communities, because of national surplus of hospital beds. Also difficult to estimate directly on a routine basis. Rough check of capacity relative to demand should suffice in most places.
	11. Change in duration and severity of congestion.	Too difficult and too much information needed to estimate routinely compared with estimating average travel times.
	12. Neighborhood stability or change in average tenure.	Tenure is not an end in itself; changes in it up or down may not necessarily be good or bad.
	13. Change in population distribution by age, income, religion, racial or ethnic group, occupational class, household type.	Not something to be maximized or minimized, as are other impacts. It is intermediate variable influencing conditions reflected by other measures. However, some communities may have a particular "mix" as a goal, and may wish to use the "new mix relative to the desired mix," or the direction of change, as the measure.
	14. Change in percent of people who perceive their neighborhood as too crowded.	Seems difficult to predict this impact, more so than some of the other measures, even qualitatively without further research on how different people interpret different densities in various settings.
	15. Change in population density.	An intermediate factor: arrangement of space and not just persons per acre is important. Effects of increased density on crowdedness of public facilities is reflected in other measures (on transportation, recreation, schools, stores, etc.).

be surveyed to assess more localized effects. Computer models of traffic distribution might be needed to estimate effects of development on areawide travel times, whereas simple back-of-the-envelope calculations may suffice for changes in travel times on roads nearest the proposed development.

To help ensure consideration of both localized and areawide effects, one can explicitly provide columns of a checklist for recording impacts at each scale, or even use two separate measures altogether. The former method was used in Indianapolis for initial review of measurements.

Project (or Incremental) Versus Planning (or Cumulative) Impacts

Some measures generally make more sense for evaluating cumulative effects of developments, comprehensive plans, or the effects of large developments than for evaluating the effects of small, individual developments.[7] A 100-home subdivision causes minor impacts on air quality either directly or indirectly, but collectively a number of such developments can cause major effects. However, even a relatively small development may cause significant communitywide effect if, for example, it negatively affects the environment of a major recreational facility, or if it includes a new type of facility or service not previously available in the community. Therefore the measurement list is *not* subdivided into measures for as-

---

7. Large developments in this context include large buildings on small tracts as well as developments that are large in area.

sessing cumulative effects and for planning uses versus measures for incremental effects from individual developments, since most measures could apply to either situation. However, Exhibit 3 does show which measures are *most likely* to be applicable to project reviews and which to planning or cumulative effects; this helps illustrate that in most reviews many measurements are likely to be quickly dismissed after an initial scan.

Residential Versus Commercial and Industrial Measures

Residential, industrial, and commercial types of development generally each give rise to a set of concerns not *usually* shared by the others. But in a given situation, impact measures normally thought of only in terms of one type of development may apply to others as well. For example, commercial development in the central business district may affect the pleasantness and use of small parks used for lunchtime relaxation, though recreation impact analyses often are thought of only for residential development. Also, each type of development may induce development of the other types. For example, new industry often attracts new residential development. Thus the secondary impacts of industrial development may be the same as the primary impacts of residential development.

Exhibit 3 indicates the measures most *usually* applicable for residential and commercial/industrial development. Again, it is emphasized that each measure on the list should be considered at least briefly for every development.

IV. CLIENTELE GROUPS

The impacts of development do not fall evenly across a community. As a result of changes in land use, benefits are enjoyed and losses are suffered in various ways and to various degrees by many different groups—such as the owners of the development site, nearby residents, commercial interests, and persons being displaced.

When development proposals are being reviewed by officials, some of the affected groups and individuals present arguments pro and con. These persons who have the time, awareness, know-how, and economic wherewithal to come forward may not represent all of the numerous groups having an important stake in the decisions. For example, low-income families and residents or small businesses just beyond the immediate neighborhood of the development site often do not have advocates at the hearings to represent their views and interests.

Evaluations of development, therefore, should not be limited to estimating community-wide impacts. They should also attempt to identify significant impacts on distinct clientele groups within the community, and preferably on groups outside the community as well.

Identifying impacts on various clientele groups should help clarify how the beneficial and detrimental effects of development are distributed and prevent a negative effect on one group from being offset by a positive impact on another. The negative impact may not be noticed if the impacts are reported as an average across all groups. This approach also may help officials to identify as-

pects of proposals which require modification before plans should be approved. Over the long run, it should help indicate when the burdens posed by development, instead of being shared uniformly, are being borne to too large an extent by particular groups. Impact analysis by clientele groups might also serve to further the dialogue between decision makers and citizens although explicitness may carry its own set of potential difficulties.[1]

For various land use proposals, different sets of clientele groups need to be considered. The pertinent groups depend on the type, size, and location of the development. The clientele groups that follow in outline form (see also Exhibit 5) are merely suggestive or illustrative of the ones that may be appropriate in any given situation. The clientele groups are described briefly. Some of the issues that merit consideration for these groups are listed; in most cases the link between these issues and the impact measures discussed earlier should be obvious. The assessments from the perspective of clientele groups will be more valuable to officials if the size of each group for which impacts are reported is indicated in summary charts for decision makers.

---

1. The mechanisms for increasing public involvement in land use planning, with particular attention to the balancing of active interest groups, affected interest groups, and the general public, have been studied by Nelson M. Rosenbaum of The Urban Institute. See Nelson M. Rosenbaum, "Citizen Involvement in Land Use Governance: Issues and Methods," The Urban Institute, Washington, D.C., 1976.

EXHIBIT 5

CLIENTELE GROUPS POTENTIALLY AFFECTED BY DEVELOPMENT

Physical Proximity

Persons living or working on the land proposed for development

Persons living or working immediately adjacent to proposed development

Persons in neighborhoods surrounding the proposed development

Persons within commuting distance (one hour by public transit, for example) from proposed commercial and industrial developments

Business Relationship

Builders, realtors, bankers, and others directly involved in the development

Owners and managers of businesses or property in the neighborhood

Political Jurisdiction

Citizens of local jurisdiction containing the development

Citizens of immediately adjacent jurisdictions and of entire metropolitan area

Citizens of the state and nation

Socioeconomic and Demographic

Age groups

Racial and ethnic groups

Persons of various income levels, from poor to affluent

Other Interest Groups

Tourists

Land owners

Others

The Long-Term Public Interest

All present groupings over time

Future generations

NOTE: This list of population segments that merit consideration is illustrative and is not all-inclusive for every situation. Many other categories will be readily apparent within the context of specific impact measures. For example, in considering transportation impacts, an important distinction to make is between persons and families with and without automobiles.

The groupings listed are not formal organizations, associations, lobby groups, or the like. Rather, they are categories of people or interest groups that are likely to be affected in different ways by development.

A. GROUPINGS BY PHYSICAL PROXIMITY TO THE DEVELOPMENT

1. Persons currently living or working on land to be developed.

Issues: Availability, accessibility, quality, and cost of relocation housing. Earnings at new jobs. Disruption of social ties. Changing schools for children. Relative satisfaction with the neighborhood in likely new locations.

2. Persons living or working on land adjacent to the development.

Issues: Almost all measures (Exhibit 3) are relevant for this group.

3. Persons living or working in neighborhoods around or near the development.

Issues: Most measures are relevant for neighborhoods—which may be defined by well-mapped boundaries (as in the case of neighborhood service areas), by socioeconomic characteristics of residents, or by proximity to the development, such as "10 minutes walking distance." Traffic, crime, air and water pollution, and crowding of major recreation facilities are among effects that may spill over into several neighborhoods. Impacts on noise, views, sociability, and privacy tend to be more localized (but this should be checked against the size and design of the specific proposal).

4. Persons within commuting distance or usage range of the development.

Issues: Those in this group vary according to the type of development. For a work center, the people included are those within the locally acceptable commuting distance or time—for example, one hour by public or private transportation. For a regional shopping center or amusement park, the people may include those in a much larger area. Note that the number of people within commuting distance cannot fairly be assessed until the effects of the development itself on public transit service, new roads, and traffic congestion are estimated. Note also that the area under discussion may include most or all of a metropolitan area and, in some instances, multistate areas. Among the many relevant measures for commercial or industrial developments are changes in employment, recreation, shopping availability, travel times, and pollution along commuter corridors. Residential developments need to be assessed in terms of available housing relative to job locations.

B. GROUPINGS BY BUSINESS RELATIONSHIPS TO THE DEVELOPMENTS

1. Businessmen directly involved in the development, such as builders, realtors, and bankers.

Issues: Businessmen may be concerned with a wide range of economic, social, and environmental changes that will affect the profitability and safety of their investment and their reputation in the community. Most impact measures, not simply the economic ones, are of interest.

2. Owners and managers of businesses or property in the neighborhood.

Issues: Number and mix of potential customers, new business competition, public safety, property values, quality of public services, and environmental impacts.

C. THE LONG-TERM PUBLIC INTEREST

Issues: Considering this group focuses attention on future generations and on all groupings over time. Enduring impacts on the physical environment, waste of natural resources, tax trends, pollution, wildlife, landmarks, and aesthetics all assume greater importance from this perspective.

Most of what has been said about the use of impact measures in general applies to the measures when they are seen from the perspective of clientele groups. These interest groups should be used first as a checklist for a quick screening so that none are forgotten. Time and money may be conserved in evaluations by narrowing this list to smaller subsets of clientele groups likely to be affected most significantly before launching into more detailed analyses.

V. THE PRACTICAL STATE OF THE ART: A SUMMARY

A set of impact measures by itself can be useful as a guide to *qualitative* evaluation of development. But for *quantitative* evaluation, it is necessary to define a set of data collection and analysis procedures for each measure. The better defined and more sound the procedures, the more likely that the information will be meaningful, comparable from case to case, and useful for defending as well as making decisions. In effect, the data collection procedures provide another level of definition for the measures.

Data collection procedures for each suggested measure are indicated in abbreviated form in Exhibit 3 in Chapter III. Discussion of data collection and analysis procedures for each measure is included in the detailed reports in this series, as previously noted.

The sections below characterize the state of the art for each group of impact areas, note methodologies common to many measurement areas, and discuss baseline data needs. Obviously this cannot have the richness that the individual reports in each area have, and has the risk of all generalizations.

GENERAL STATE OF THE ART

The current state of the art in impact evaluation is somewhat mixed. Areas that many think are on solid technical grounds, such as estimates of pollution, transportation, and fiscal impacts, are softer, more complex, have less validated methodologies, and require more value judgments than their associated computer models suggest. On the other hand, areas usually thought of as "soft" and too nebulous to meet legal tests, such as estimates of impacts on neighborhood aesthetics, use of informal outdoor space, shopping, and privacy may be more approachable than one expects, at least in some common situations. Decision makers and their staffs should therefore carefully question the soundness of the so-called "hard data" or "technical facts," and not despair too quickly over explicitly estimating social impacts of great concern to the citizenry.

Below are capsule summaries of the state of the art in each impact area listed in Exhibit 3. The Roman numerals correspond to Exhibit 3; a few exceptions have been made in grouping specific measures under the headings because common techniques permitted briefer discussions. Again the reader is referred to the detailed reports in this series for an expanded discussion.

I. Local Economy

Fiscal Impacts

Estimating revenues from new development seems straightforward so long as the approximate income level of new residents, property value, and sales volume of new businesses can in turn be estimated at least roughly. There are relatively inexpensive computer models and "cookbook" procedures for such estimates that are often good enough for first order approximations.

However, a large percentage of local revenues comes from property taxes. Taxes are affected by changes in property values, and the effects of development on property values are poorly understood quantitatively, though there is considerable theory on the subject. Thus, although short-term revenues from a proposed development can be approximated, the long-term revenues and the change in revenues from the rest of the community are probably beyond the state of the art to estimate routinely or with adequate reliability.

Estimating public operating expenses from new development is straightforward *if* the assumption that the new development will lead to the same per capita expenses as currently exist in the rest of the community is valid. However, when this assumption does not hold, as is usually the case, the analysis becomes more judgmental. New households often have different characteristics than the average community household with respect to important characteristics such as income, number of children and age of household members.

Allocating public capital expenses among new and existing households also presents major conceptual problems about which there is not common agreement among economists or the courts. For example, should one allocate old capital plant, such as schools with available seating capacity, to the new development in proportion to the number of seat-years it uses? Or should just the incremental cost of the seat-years be used, thereby giving full benefits of any economies of scale to the new development? Should only out-of-pocket expenses be used, and so forth.

Secondary effects of development on fiscal flows also are not well enough understood quantitatively. These include, for example, the fiscal impacts of residential development likely to be stimulated by a proposed industrial development, or business stimulated by new residential and industrial development.

Thus although there are many approaches to fiscal analysis and many models and other methods currently used by local governments, the results must be used with care. Sensitivity analyses—estimating outputs as various inputs or assumptions are varied—should be considered when estimating potential fiscal impacts (and other impacts, too) rather than relying on a single computation to produce a single best estimate where the above complicating factors are likely to be significant.

Private Economy Impacts: Employment and Wealth

Estimating *employment impacts* means more than just counting the number of new jobs in a proposed development. Some of the "new jobs" may be jobs transferred from elsewhere in the community and thus not a net increase. Some new jobs may be filled from outside the community, and thus not reduce unemployment within the community. The total number of jobs likely to be created in the public and private sector can be estimated. Much more difficult is estimating how many of these jobs will fall to the community, and what dent this may make in current unemployment and underemployment. Rough estimates can be made by considering whether the mix of new jobs likely to fall to current community residents matches profiles of unemployed or underemployed workers' skills. The problem here is the level of detail at which this analysis can be done: the skill levels of the new jobs and the existing availability of suitable workers are not always well defined at the time of analysis.

There are no "standard" approaches to estimating changes in *land values*, though in some situations a very rough estimate of the direction of change and the order of magnitude of change may be possible. There is a considerable body of economic theory on this subject but few operational models analogous, say, to fiscal impact models except for a few research studies. However, individual communities may be able to predict changes based on their past experience for residential development.

II. Natural Environment Impacts

There are several manual and several computerized *air quality* models available for local government use today. The manual techniques yield inexpensive, quick approximations, but are better for estimating long-term changes in pollutant concentrations from overall growth than for localized areas. The computerized models tend to be more expensive (tens of thousands of dollars) to set up but cost much less than that for each repeated use. Some of the manual and some of the computer models have been validated with fairly good success; others of each type have not been adequately tested or have been found not to be very reliable. Local governments should be wary of which particular models they use and whether or not they have been validated, especially when using outside consultants for the models.

Although much research is devoted to the subject, the health impacts of various air pollution levels are still uncertain, especially long term effects. This limits the confidence behind estimates of impacts on people, especially for concentrations below current standards.

Water pollution impacts can be estimated fairly accurately only for a very few pollutants and under limited conditions. Water quality models tend to be expensive, and still require judgments to interpret the potential health and recreational effects of various levels of pollutant concentrations, because of the uncertainty in concentrations likely to cause health hazards.

Simple techniques for estimating *flood frequency and magnitude* are available but tend to be unreliable. While more complex and expensive models are presumably more accurate, their degree of accuracy has not been well established. Studies undertaken by the Corps of Engineers under the National Disaster Act may improve the quality of these models.

Methods for estimating the *supply of water* for consumption are analogous to those used for estimating flood frequency and volume, for surface water. Only qualitative assessments are normally possible for underground water sources. Fortunately, some of the more complex water models can be used for estimating flooding, water pollution, and water consumption impacts, with some resulting economy of scale.

Wildlife and vegetation inventories can be made with adequate accuracy, but predicting impacts on wildlife numbers is still largely dependent on the judgment of wildlife experts. Nevertheless, changes in habitats coupled with that judgment can give reasonably good guidance for land use decision making. Graduate students can be used for establishing current inventories. This important area seems more approachable than its infrequent inclusion in impact evaluation by local government might suggest.

Primary effects on amount of vegetation are relatively straightforward to assess; longer term impacts due to air pollution, the introduction of competitive species, and so forth are much more difficult to estimate.

Noise impacts from changes in traffic volume and mix can be estimated reasonably accurately using simple models. Noise from other sources is more difficult to estimate quantitatively, but it too can be at least roughly estimated which is usually sufficient for decision making.

Risk from *natural disasters* other than flooding, such as earthquakes and landslides, can be estimated at least qualitatively. Maps indicating certain types of hazards are available for some areas of the country.

Estimation of impacts on scarce resources is another impact area that tends not to receive adequate attention. Estimating impacts on availability of *scarce resources* such as agricultural land (or mineral deposits) is straightforward to do superficially. But it is difficult to estimate the impacts on total food (or mineral) production potential because of continual improvements in production technology and the reclamation of resources such as farm land elsewhere in the country.

III. Aesthetics and Cultural Values

Aesthetics is basically subjective. The question is, first, how to systematically obtain subjective judgments of the citizens, and then to determine to what extent they can be predicted. Current perceptions of neighborhood *attractiveness* can be collected using a survey of a random sample of neighborhood residents. The survey can help identify features held particularly attractive or especially undesirable. At the minimum, a proposed development can be evaluated with respect to what positive and negative features it will remove. The new development itself in the context of its setting may be rated by current residents using visual simulations in the form of drawings, 3-D models, or retouched photos; the latter seem most practical. The use of photos as stand-ins for actual scenes has been validated for landscapes and recreational settings, but not for urban settings, though it appears promising. Computerized 3-D simulations and holographic displays are potentially useful but still in early research stages and too expensive for routine use.

The degree to which *views* from households or

businesses are blocked or expanded can be identified in part by simple geometric analyses.

Changes in the availability and accessibility of *landmarks* is a matter of simple fact. Their importance may already be indicated in historic registers; if not, local experts may be queried, or citizen surveys can be used to get a rough rating. Since for most areas landmarks will only occasionally be affected, the survey effort involved may be quite tolerable. It is also relatively simple to identify the rarity of the landmark and distance to the nearest similar example.

IV. Public and Private Services[1]

For *hospital services,* the availability and response time for emergency care may be computed with the use of maps. Unless the proposed development itself includes emergency care facilities, effects of development on availability of emergency care for the rest of the community are usually negligible. Effects on availability and quality of non-emergency hospital services can only be grossly assessed in terms of potential number of beds needed versus existing area supply. This should suffice in most areas, so long as the general condition of excess bed capacity continues.

Predicting changes in *fire* and *crime* rates is generally beyond the present state of the art except that one may make the assumption that proposed developments will experience about the same rates as do existing land uses of the same types. Predicting how a new commercial center near a residential neighborhood may attract crime away from the residential neighborhood or bring crime to it is an example of more complex questions that are beyond the state of the art. Expert ratings of likely hazards presented is about the best one can do for estimating "end" impacts on the existing community. Intermediate impacts such as changes in frequency of police patrols, in physical conditions likely to affect feelings of security, in accessibility to fire apparatus, and so forth are readily identified but somewhat difficult to interpret in terms of changes in hazards presented.

Changes in accessibility of both formal and informal *recreation* facilities are straightforward

---

1. Drinking water is discussed above, under "Natural Environment Impacts."

to estimate. At the opposite end of the spectrum, changes in citizen satisfaction and usage of facilities are difficult to estimate with any confidence. As a middle course, similar to estimating aesthetic impacts (and other social impacts as well), it seems feasible to identify (a) current neighborhood usage and satisfaction with informal and formal recreational opportunities and reasons for satisfaction or dissatisfaction, using citizen surveys, direct observation, and diaries; and (b) physical changes to recreational facilities, environment, or accessibility that may affect recreational opportunity or enjoyment. Inferences can then be drawn about the likely impacts on satisfaction or usage. For example, a development that significantly raises the noise level at a park site will probably decrease enjoyability of that site. It may not affect attendance, however, if there are no nearby alternatives, unless conditions get extreme. Increased traffic through streets in which children play may force them to use more distant sites, or to continue current use at higher risk, or to eliminate these activities altogether. Although one cannot be sure of which end will result, the outcomes can be bounded and interpreted in light of the extent of current use, current enjoyment, and alternative sites and activities available. Although the potential for success is not clear, local governments may try to develop a set of case histories of before-and-after effects of development on recreation (and other social conditions) so that projections of citizen satisfaction and usage based on past analogies can be used to supplement other approaches. We have not identified any government currently doing this for more than a rare special study, however.

Immediate changes in *school* accessibility, crowdedness, and rescheduling of children by shifts are relatively straightforward to estimate. Long-term crowdedness depends on final decisions—whether the presence of added students triggers new school construction. Impacts of development on the quality of education are far beyond the current state of the art; in fact, measuring the quality of education is a highly controversial issue even for existing school and community conditions.

Estimating impacts on *transportation* will probably meet with mixed success. In order to estimate changes in travel times between key origins and destinations, the expected characteristics of the future residents/employees of the proposed development can be used to make assumptions about their travel behavior. The impact of the new trips throughout the transportation network can then be simulated using relatively elaborate transportation models. But the accuracy of the resulting estimates may be low and difficult to determine. However, expected delays and congestion on local streets can be estimated more easily and with greater confidence.

The estimates of impacts on local parking conditions would appear to be straightforward although the suggested approach has not been tested. Changes in accessibility to mass transit are likewise easily estimated. Safety impacts, on the other hand, must be based on a largely subjective analysis of safety hazards and analogies to other examples where changes in traffic have been compared with changes in accident rates.

Estimated changes in accessibility of *shopping* may be measured directly. Estimating changes in household satisfaction with shopping opportunities has problems similar to those for recreation, and again fallback measures such as the change in the variety of shopping opportunity and physical conditions of shopping areas are needed.

The degree to which the availability of *energy* service to the existing residents will be affected by new development is very difficult to estimate. Somewhat more feasible is to rate the relative efficiency with which the proposed development will be heated and cooled in the case of residential and commercial developments, or with which goods will be produced in the case of industrial developments. However, the analysis requires detailed specification or assumptions of building design and construction or of the manufacturing processes to be used—information which is not usually available at the time an application for a zoning change is filed.

Changes in *housing* supply (number of residential units by type) can be compared to housing needs. The needs are estimated according to assumptions about the type and price of housing affordable by (and presumably desired by) households of different income groups, household size, age, and stage of life cycle. Estimating housing demand is also complicated by the influence of regional housing supply and demand on that of a particular jurisdiction. Historical patterns of usage can be used to estimate roughly how much of newly created housing stock will be available to persons in neighboring or remote jurisdictions, unless these jurisdictions have undergone sharp increases in their industrial employment or if available land in them is "filling up."

Estimating changes in housing supply has the complication that the housing chain (or "filtering process") created by a new housing unit is not adequately understood. People in the community moving from an existing unit to a new one leave behind them one which in turn may attract someone from perhaps yet another unit in the community, who leaves his to someone else, and so on. What happens at the end of the chain is often fuzzy. Whether the least expensive unit at the end of the chain becomes abandoned or attracts someone from within or without the jurisdiction is usually not known. Studying housing chains is vital, especially for older communities where there is much "downward filtering" of units.

V. Other Social Impacts

The number of residents, workers, and businesses to be *displaced* by new development is readily identifiable. Simple surveys of people to be displaced can help identify their degree of dissatisfaction or satisfaction, given the specifics of compensation and aid they are given for finding alternative locations. The methodological question here is whether answers to surveys are likely to be honest in this context.

Identifying special *physical hazards* created by development (in addition to traffic hazards) is largely judgmental.

Changes in *social interaction* patterns or perceptions of the adequacy of *friendliness* of neighborhoods cannot be forecast with present knowledge in most cases. Again, a viable approach is first to identify current baseline conditions, using citizen surveys; identify expected changes in physical barriers to interactions (e.g., highways which split neighborhoods, changes in people mix and changes in available settings for social activities). Then impacts may be inferred. Again, local governments may eventually be able to improve forecasts of citizen satisfaction after developing a backlog of case studies on which to base projections.

Changes in the visual *privacy* or residences, as from new sightlines from a highrise into the backyards of single-family dwellings, may be estimated with simple geometric analysis. Assessing future changes in satisfaction with privacy has the same problem as in projecting satisfaction for the other areas already mentioned.

Overall citizen satisfaction with one's neighborhood may not be directly projectable, but the degree of change to neighborhood elements likely to affect satisfaction or dissatisfaction can be identified systematically, especially if baseline studies assessing reasons for satisfaction and dissatisfaction have been made.

BASELINE DATA NEEDS FOR COMPREHENSIVE IMPACT EVALUATION

To assess most types of impacts discussed above it is first necessary to establish current baseline conditions. This may be done at the time a special development is under review, or on a periodic basis independent of specific development reviews. A third option is a mix of the two: an inventory is taken of baseline conditions for community characteristics likely to be affected by developments, with additional spot analyses undertaken as needed to identify baseline conditions for characteristics only infrequently pertinent to decision making (e.g., the importance of selected landmarks). In general, if there are likely to be a large number of developments to be reviewed during a year, say in the hundreds, it will be more efficient to establish baselines for the community—or at least for the parts of the community undergoing growth—say once a year.

Many local governments today already routinely monitor environmental conditions, or have access to such data from regional or state agencies. A small but growing number are periodically monitoring citizen satisfaction with municipal services on a regular basis: Nashville, St. Petersburg, Palo Alto, and Dallas are examples. However, very few local governments assess current social conditions such as privacy, friendliness, crowdedness, or satisfaction with aesthetics and informal recreation opportunities.

Below are listed some types of baseline data needed for estimating development impacts, grouped by *techniques used* to gather the information. Baseline data would be gathered in these "bundles" for economy of scale.[2]

Citizen Surveys

A survey of a scientifically selected random sample of citizens can be used to identify the current frequency that neighborhood facilities are used and the reasons for non-usage by specific facility, type of user, and mode of getting to it. Facilities to evaluate might include formal recreation areas such as parks, informal recreation areas such as empty lots and sidewalks, and stores. The surveys can also be used to identify current satisfaction levels with neighborhood appearance, public services, and social conditions; reasons for dissatisfaction; and neighborhood features felt to be especially good or bad. This valuable information can be collected in a systematic way and is not easily obtained by any other means. Citizen surveys can further serve to provide information to planners for long-range development of a neighborhood. An example of a survey questionnaire for assessing social impacts is given in Christensen.[3]

In addition to establishing baseline conditions, citizen surveys may be used to identify citizen preferences for types of development desired in their neighborhood, and types to be avoided. Specific comparisons among various proposed development alternatives or a proposed development versus no development may also be undertaken. Care must be taken, however, to describe clearly the proposed development to survey respondents.

Mini-surveys consisting of just a few questions may also be used effectively to establish baseline conditions in the area of a proposed development. They may be used as a substitute for broader surveys or to supplement questions on larger surveys, probing for additional detail or filling in gaps left by the general survey. For example, Indianapolis on one occasion used a short survey to determine

---

2. This repeats some of the information discussed in the state of the art section above but it is grouped in a different way.

3. Kathleen Christensen, *Social Impacts of Land Development*, op. cit.

neighborhood usage of some local stores scheduled for displacement by a proposed development. Citizens within a specified radius (5 or 6 blocks) of the proposed development were surveyed, and in this case a very small random sample, about 17 respondents, sufficed because the response was so uniform. This type of survey can be designed and conducted in one or two days by one person; in Indianapolis, one interviewer surveyed 17 persons in one afternoon and, since virtually all the responses were in the same direction, the accuracy was sufficient.

Surveys may be conducted in person, by telephone, or by mail. Costs tend to decrease and reliability to increase in that order. In-person surveys typically cost $10–$20 (in 1975) per completed interview taking 30 to 40 minutes. The number of citizens to be surveyed depends on the number of citizen groupings for which separate ratings are desired and on the reliability needed. Roughly speaking, 50 to 100 interviews for each group are needed at a minimum. To get information on each of five areas of a community, one might use 500 interviews, 100 per district. Survey data can be compared for different districts or neighborhoods, and for a given neighborhood over time to identify problem areas. Surveys before and after development may help identify impacts, with the lessons applied to future development evaluations.

Physical Measurements

Water and air pollution concentrations already are measured in many communities where potential problems may arise. Noise levels are much less frequently measured on a routine basis, but noise meters are relatively inexpensive and, with some training in how to choose sampling locations and frequencies, easy to use. In a society with growing noise problems, increased attention to noise measurement seems justified.

Physical Inventories

Inventories of public facilities are kept by virtually all communities, often in the form of maps. Inventories of shopping areas also are usually available, but not always at a level of detail needed for neighborhood decision making. Inventories of the abundance and diversity of wildlife and vegetation are much less frequently available on a routine basis but they are increasing; graduate students from local universities often can be called upon to make the inventories, which require special identification skills. A number of cities, most notably Dallas and San Francisco, have pioneered in making inventories of aesthetic resources such as views, attractive streets, and landscaping, as well as the more common inventories of landmarks.

Economic Data from Census and Municipal Records

These are needed for general planning as well as development evaluation. Data needs include revenues and typical expenditures for each type of new land development, by household characteristics. Numbers of persons unemployed and underemployed, jurisdiction of residence for employees in the jurisdiction, and migration patterns all are needed to estimate impacts on unemployment. Changes in land values are needed for estimating changes in wealth. Profiles of housing stock by price, income distributions, percent of unrented and unoccupied housing in satisfactory condition, and of the disposition of lower-priced housing at the end of the housing chain are needed to help estimate how well new housing satisfies existing demand for housing.

In addition to the above baseline data, additional information will need to be collected for many measures at the time a particular proposed development is under review. Some data already collected in baseline studies will have to be collected in greater detail. For example, it may not be sufficient to know that children in a suburban subdivision or in cul-de-sacs generally play in the street; study of a particular street about to be converted into a through street, and the alternatives to it, might have to be investigated.

VI. USING AN IMPACT MEASUREMENT SYSTEM

The systematic use of impact measurements is not a rigid concept. Though it was developed originally for reviewing individual development projects, it can be used in the preparation and review of comprehensive or area plans as well. An impact measurement checklist can be used by many different actors involved in land use decision making and it may fit into many different places in the decision process.

This chapter, supplemented by the next one, discusses potential uses and users. It also discusses constraints on usage and some key analysis issues pertinent to formulating development review policies. Important uses of measurement systems are apparent for many governments, large and small, though the details may vary a great deal from one to another.

DIFFERENT USERS

In the course of evaluating individual developments or comprehensive plans, impact checklists may be used by any or all of the various parties involved in the decision.

Use by Planning Staff

The staff may include as part of each development evaluation an estimate of impacts using the measures on a pre-defined list. The development would be at least briefly and qualitatively reviewed against each measure, to make an initial judgment as to whether a non-trivial positive or negative impact is likely on that particular element. If a potential significant impact exists, specific staff members may be assigned to undertake a more detailed analysis of that particular item.

The staff may use an impact checklist only internally, to help structure their reviews, but not presenting data to the decision makers as "measurements" per se. Alternatively, a set of measures jointly agreed to by staff and decision making bodies may lead to the use of the checklist as part of hearings or other formal reviews. (See sections below for more on use by decision makers.)

The staff may use checklists for both "quickie" analyses and detailed analyses, and for small as well as large developments. The use of a checklist for every development obviously precludes detailed analysis on every item in every review, as previously stressed. Most measures can be used to describe impacts in rough qualitative terms as well as in detail. Thus, the list may guide analysis even if the analysis is brief and only aims at approximations. Examples of staff use of checklists for rough qualitative and detailed quantitative evaluations are given in Chapter VII.

If a measurement system is not to be used in toto, it still may be useful to improve estimation procedures for some selected impact areas. One might develop natural environment measures and associated estimation procedures first, then others at a later time. Various measures and procedures may be added as staff resources and "adequate" methodology become available.[1] This poses some problems of potential imbalances in level of detail of data presented for various types of impacts, but those imbalances are likely to exist whatever evaluation approach is used.

Use by Zoning and Planning Directors

Planning directors, zoning administrators, or others in charge of development reviews may personally use the impact checklist to see whether each important potential impact has been considered in the review, regardless of the form the review takes. That is, even if a narrative staff report is used, reference to the checklist can help make it complete.

Zoning administrators often have authority to make decisions on certain types of zoning adjustments, such as variances or special exceptions; the specific powers vary from community to community. Cases may number as many as 1,000 per year, as in Phoenix. The impact checklist can be used by these decision makers to organize their reviews and guard against oversights. (See remarks by Phoenix Zoning Administrator in Chapter IX, and example of impacts identified in Example 3, Chapter VII.)

Use by Commissions, Boards, and Councils

Decision making bodies may require each proposal or some classes of proposals they review to be evaluated against an impact checklist jointly agreed to with the planning staff, with the results presented to them in a standard format to make comparisons from one proposal to another easier. This helps establish a "language" for communications between staff and decision makers and helps them avoid misunderstandings. Of course this takes an initial investment in agreeing to a list of measures and set of definitions that are workable and understandable. And it takes good faith by both decision makers and staffs to adapt to an ongoing impact measurement system or to devise a new one quickly enough to be of use for the major part of political terms.

---

1. Each jurisdiction must decide what is "adequate" for its purposes—something that is fully validated, something that is better than nothing, or some point between these extremes.

While some decision makers like a fixed format, others abhor it. They voice concern that evaluations based on a complete set of measures may lead to undue detail in analyzing small developments or attention to issues that could be quickly set aside, with a waste of money and time of all concerned. They are also concerned that reviews will not be free to take into account unexpected issues that may crop up, or considerations that have not been adequately captured by the formal set of measures. For example, where development is seen as needed for the image of the community, or to increase stability of a way of life, or to improve business opportunities in the future, a formal system of impact measures may not adequately portray these concerns. However, proper use of a measurement system entails choosing the right level of analysis for each measure in each review, and using the system only as one tool in an overall review. Other issues that are not reflected by the predetermined measurement system can and should be brought in as part of the review narrative.

A second major mode by which decision makers may use the measurement system is simply to use it informally themselves to help guide their own evaluation of a case, to see if staff analysis is complete, and to suggest questions to put to the various parties. Sometimes a planning staff may be encouraged to do a better job of analysis in the first place when they know an astute decision maker will be systematically probing their reviews.

Other Users

Citizens may use the system in the same way as just described for decision makers—to help ensure that all potentially important impacts are considered. Citizen groups may also use an impact measurement checklist to help guide their own analysis of a situation, and to collect information in a more systematic and possibly more persuasive way. Citizens often compete with staff for the ear of the decision maker. A more professional approach may help get adequate hearing.

Developers and other business interests related to land use decisions have a stake in seeing that the benefits of development are considered. Often the positive side—the economic benefits, improved services or shopping, housing stock, and so forth—are not adequately presented. The measurement list of course is not the only way to approach this problem, but it can help assure that all impacts get considered by all parties and that the review of positive effects is viewed as routine, not a political move.

Higher level government agencies (regional, state, and federal) are another class of potential users of impact measurement systems. Florida, for example, has a very detailed list of data (which could easily be called "measurements") that is required for each "development of regional impact." Federal and other state environmental impact statements often require information on a number of items, some of which are specific "measures," but more often they are not completely defined nor stated in the form of measures.

The *courts* are yet another potential user of impact measurements, either to help establish facts of what a development under litigation may do to the community, or to test the consistency from one review to another.

Establishing *a community of users* has a potential for obtaining some of the greatest advantages from measurement checklists. Phoenix, for example, has attempted to get all parties involved in land use decisions and planning thinking comprehensively and quantitatively. As part of their evolution of development reviews, they distributed copies of the initial report in this series, which included a suggested checklist of measures, to the city council, planning staff, and members of a number of citizens groups which participate in land use decision making.[2]

TYPES OF USES AND HOW THEY FIT IN THE DECISION PROCESS

A local government may develop an impact measurement system for use in any of five major roles, discussed below. In most situations, the same system could apply.

Reviewing Individual Proposed Developments

The bread and butter use of a measurement system, the one motivating this study, is the review

---

2. Although the very attempt is interesting in itself, and the initial reactions by the mayor, zoning administrator, and city council were positive, it is too early to tell whether the effect will be lasting and truly contribute toward improved decision making. (See the final chapter for a summary of the Phoenix experience.)

of individual development proposals. It is usually not sufficient to assume that if a development fits in with the master plan for an area, it should be approved. Master plans rarely if ever contain enough detail to negate the need for at least a brief look at localized impact of developments. Broader, communitywide impacts such as overall air pollution, water quality, water availability, and travel times *may* be adequately evaluated by checking compliance with master plans, so long as these matters were considered in formulating the master plans and the plans are not out of date. But if the master plan for an area is five to ten years old, and conditions such as emission controls on automobiles and automobile per capita usage have changed in ways not expected, it may not adequately reflect air quality or other areawide considerations. Likewise, as the population mix and local and national mores change, plans may be more rapidly outdated than earlier envisioned.

For communities that update comprehensive plans say at least once every five years, it may suffice to occasionally study cumulative effects of development to see if plans need updating, or to review an occasional development in detail to see if the assumptions about household usage of facilities, water effluents attributable to new development, and so forth are still valid.

Even where comprehensive plans are relatively up-to-date and adequate for checking communitywide effects, potential localized impacts on neighborhood traffic congestion, aesthetics, privacy, access to neighborhood formal and informal recreation centers, etc. still need to be checked.

A measurement system may be used to evaluate various types of proposed zoning changes or adjustments—*rezonings, variances,* or *special exceptions.* The level of detail of information available, the effort justified by staff, and legal requirements and constraints may be different for each type of change. For example, rezonings for planned unit developments (PUDs) generally have much more detailed information on the site plan, the types of industry or residences planned, and much more discretion left to the staff and decision makers than do other types of rezonings. In both Phoenix and Indianapolis, the consensus of the planning staff was that at one time or another most classes of impacts were important in each type of review, and that it did not seem to pay to develop separate lists for each type of review (that is, variance, rezoning, etc.). In situations such as that faced by Montgomery County, however, where there are tight legal constraints on considerations allowed in making individual zoning map amendments, a much more extensive list might be considered for PUDs than for other types of rezoning reviews.

Different levels of analysis often are appropriate at different points in the decision process—initial informal review, formal staff review, planning commission decision, appeals, etc. Each government should identify what level of detail is typically available at each stage of decision making, and what types of considerations are legal in determining measures to use. Clearly a rezoning in which the development owners have to specify only the general category of industrial use contemplated cannot be reviewed for impact on visual attractiveness in the same way as can a detailed site plan for a PUD.

Evaluating Comprehensive Plans

As indicated in Exhibit 3, many impact measures seem suitable for evaluating comprehensive plans as well as individual projects. For some types of impacts, especially economic and environmental effects, it may be even more appropriate to evaluate them cumulatively as part of planning than as part of individual projects. Planning has fewer legal constraints regarding what may or may not be considered than development reviews, but usually cannot consider as detailed a level of impacts as can development reviews.

Measurements can help translate some of the features of colored charts typical of planning into terms that will aid understanding of the different types of land use and kinds of community they imply. It is usually quite difficult to communicate the ideas behind comprehensive plans to the citizens in terms of end impacts on them. The reasoning and care a staff may put into seeing that each residential neighborhood has certain facilities may be lost in the awesome color patterns and details of an overall map. For example, the percent of citizens within a quarter mile walk of a neighborhood park, the expected travel times between various sections of the community, and expected air quality levels are difficult to grasp

from maps alone. Nor is it possible for most citizens—and perhaps decision makers—to tell if these matters were taken into account in the preparation of the plans. Perhaps most importantly, the use of measures may encourage planners not already doing so to examine more carefully and comprehensively the likely impacts from their plans.

Of course, the estimation of some types of impacts, such as the patterns of future development likely under a given plan, still are matters of judgment and are not going to be helped much by using a set of measures. It must be kept in mind that the system of measures is only one tool for approaching the evaluation problem.

The use of measures for evaluating plans is of course nothing new. Though most local governments do not have a formal checklist applied for each plan, many evaluate key aspects of their plans quantitatively. But there seems to be considerable room for improvement even in some of the most advanced governments.

Linking Planning to Project Review

In many planning organizations, especially in larger communities, the long-range planning staff responsible for developing comprehensive plans is separate from the development review section. Sometimes this separation is wider than intended. Those reviewing developments should be keeping in mind the longer-term interests of the community, as expressed in part by comprehensive plans; and comprehensive planners must consider the changing realities of the community which result from one by one development decisions. While there is probably broad agreement on this, the ideal often gets lost amidst daily pressures on both the development reviewers and planners. One potential way to keep the two groups working together is to have both use a similar set of impact measures so they will share a common approach, measurement language, and impact analysis tools. An even stronger tie can be developed by incorporating targets for appropriate measures into the comprehensive plans themselves, as discussed further below.

Measures such as "the percent of population within x miles of a transit stop," "the percent within x miles of a neighborhood park for young children," the "percent exposed to noise levels near their homes above y decibels at night," and "the shortfall of housing units needed by price range" can be used by both groups. Even measures based on citizen perceptions, such as the "percent of citizens finding their neighborhood attractive," or the "percent finding their neighborhood a good place to live," can be monitored by both groups.

Use of Impact Targets and "Budgets" in Comprehensive Plans

Quantitative targets and "performance budgets" built into comprehensive plans are another potentially important way of linking planning to project review, and perhaps of improving the plans.

For many types of impacts, the incremental change brought about by individual developments is measurable but insignificant for all but the largest developments. This typically applies to impacts on air and water quality, wildlife abundance, travel times, fiscal flows, and employment. It is often impractical to compute *cumulative* effects to date for each development proposal, and local government often is not allowed to consider the cumulative effect of groups of proposed developments together when making one by one decisions.

Were planning a perfect process, the comparison of a proposal with the designated zoning would suffice for consideration of areawide effects—no computation of them would be necessary. But the assumptions on which plans are based may not continue to hold throughout the period that the plans are in effect. Also, certain effects may not have been considered or may have been compromised in the development of the plan. Finally, the range of development allowed under many zoning categories, especially commercial and industrial ones, is so broad that the community may reach a considerably different position than expected at the time of plan adoption.

One way out of these dilemmas is to incorporate into the comprehensive plan quantitative targets to be reached or ceilings to be avoided. These may be air or water quality levels, levels of employment, maximum travel times between selected origins and destinations, risks of flooding damage to be accepted, and so forth. Corresponding to each of these targets, "tipping

points" or "budgets" can be computed for intermediate variables such as: the number of new residential units per square mile or square feet of new office space that are tolerable before they cause traffic and hence travel times or noise to reach unacceptable levels; the amount of new emissions and effluents of various types tolerable in various sectors of the community before air or water quality reaches unacceptable levels; the number of acres of habitat needed for certain types of wildlife to remain abundant in the community; the number of acres of impermeable cover before flooding becomes a problem; and so forth. These can be precomputed, if necessary, using more sophisticated and expensive analysis techniques than is possible on a day to day basis.[3] For project reviews, a cumulative, running total would be kept of these intermediate variables until a tipping point is neared, allowing a margin for analysis errors. Only then, in most cases, would a more detailed analysis of areawide effects be needed for development reviews. Alternatively, approaching a tipping point might identify need for a new comprehensive plan. Exhibit 6 illustrates the concept. The running total need not be revised for literally every development. Rather, it can be done periodically for groups of development, the period depending on the rate of growth and the community's proximity to the targets or budget limits.

Targets or budgets will most likely be more suited to subareas within a community rather than to the community as a whole. Subareas often differ, for example, in the amounts of additional impervious ground cover that can be tolerated before localized flooding will occur, or in the amounts of additional traffic that can be borne on existing or scheduled road networks. Also, different environmental quality target levels would be set for residential and industrial subareas.

To simplify impact analysis, it may be possible to identify the one or two types of impacts likely to be most critical or limiting for each subarea as further development takes place. For example, it may be found in the course of developing a plan that travel time and congestion impacts

---

3. For impacts such as air pollution, simple techniques may suffice for communitywide assessments. See Keyes, op. cit., for specific alternatives.

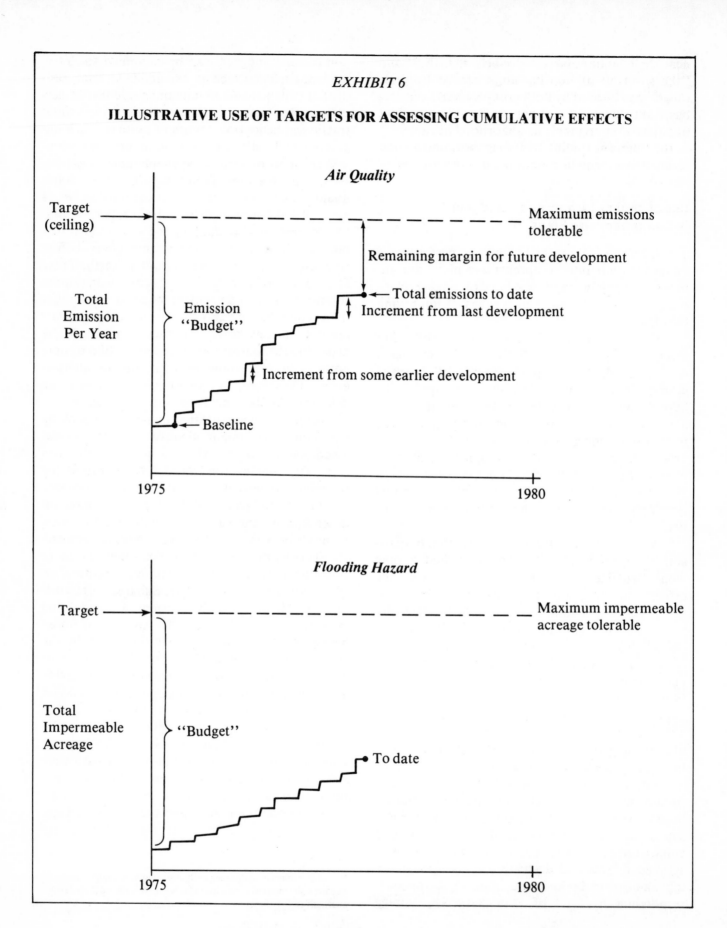

EXHIBIT 6

ILLUSTRATIVE USE OF TARGETS FOR ASSESSING CUMULATIVE EFFECTS

Air Quality

Target (ceiling) ——→ Maximum emissions tolerable

Total Emission Per Year

Emission "Budget"

Remaining margin for future development

← Total emissions to date
Increment from last development

Increment from some earlier development

← Baseline

1975   1980

Flooding Hazard

Target ——→ Maximum impermeable acreage tolerable

Total Impermeable Acreage

"Budget"

● To date

1975   1980

are apt to become intolerable long before air pollution will. Thus, as proposed development induces vehicular traffic build-up, the analysis need focus only on the first constraint likely to be exceeded—congestion.

Montgomery County, Maryland, exemplifies a sophisticated evolution toward increased use of running totals checked periodically against pre-set targets that are incorporated into adopted master plans in terms of the amounts of allowable future development. When targets are reached, these trigger more detailed analysis of problem areas. In certain high density areas of the county, for example, traffic levels are considered a key restraint and are checked whenever approximately 100,000 square feet of new building space is added. Running totals of office space added are made about every three months in times of high growth, and about every six months in slow growth. The count is based on building permit records and is calculated manually. Similar thresholds are planned for air pollution, stormwater drainage, flooding and perhaps noise pollution.

Running totals of impacts could be used in another important way. They signal in advance how much margin or "budget" is left for additional new development before the tipping point is reached. Knowing the average amount of effluents, impermeable acres, housing units, etc., usually added per new unit thus allows an estimate to be made of how many more units can be approved before an undesirable condition results.

The targets and budgets have to be readjusted or verified every so often to see if the assumptions on which they rest have changed; for example, to see if levels of private auto effluents or emissions per *existing* household are as expected.

Retrospective Analysis

A major data source for improving impact analyses, neglected by most local governments, is the development of a series of case histories of the impacts of past development. These retrospective analyses can provide data for estimating impacts of proposed developments and for helping to judge the validity of previously used predictive techniques.

The case histories preferably would be based on before-and-after studies in the neighborhood surrounding the development rather than on studies made only after development was completed.[4] They would be especially useful for estimating social impacts, for which there are no adequate models and which might best benefit from comparison with analogies in one's own community. If a number of communities undertook even a few such analyses using a common terminology, say with impact measures suggested in Exhibit 3, it might be possible to share results. One would look for consistent patterns of cause and effect. If a highrise built in a residential low-rise neighborhood sometimes created community problems but sometimes did not, that would suggest more uncertainty in estimating the impact for another proposed highrise. If in virtually every case the highrise had no significant negative effects on citizen perceptions and usage of their community, then the odds are that another highrise in a similar setting would not either. If the highrise almost always caused people to sense a loss of privacy or a decrease in attractiveness, then it is likely that another highrise in a similar situation would lead to similar results.

Case histories can use the set of measures in Exhibit 3 applied before and after development. Retrospective analysis has the great advantage of being able to use all of the preferred measures indicated, and not the proxies, if data is gathered before and after development. In general, it is much easier to measure an existing condition or set of perceptions than to predict or reconstruct them. For example, citizen satisfaction with recreation opportunities can be directly assessed using citizen surveys, whereas projecting impacts on satisfaction requires many assumptions.

Case histories might also make use of baseline data collected for long-range planning. For example, if the community is to be surveyed annually for long-range planning, some added sampling in the neighborhoods of recent developments allows comparisons between neighborhoods with and without recent developments at relatively low incremental cost.

Of course, use of case histories is fraught with dangers; situations are never identical, and all

---

4. Retrospective studies require that conditions which no longer exist must be estimated—not much easier than predicting conditions which do not yet exist.

comparisons must be made with caution. Another major problem in undertaking retrospective analyses is to separate development-related impacts from those caused by other factors such as changes in the local economy, air pollution spilling in from nearby communities, changes in the entire community's use of personal autos and so forth. Nevvertheless, these analyses seem to offer much potential for improved estimates of impacts that are difficult to predict otherwise.

Retrospective analyses may be undertaken for *community plans* as well as for individual developments. Two questions may be asked: Was the plan followed, and did predicted impacts occur as expected? Although review of past plans and current situations is commonplace as part of the planning process, often these evaluations do not focus on end concerns of the citizens, but rather on whether development moved in directions planned, changes in the composition of the population and commerce, and so forth.

Federal and State Impact Statements

The federal government, as mandated by the Natural Environment Policy Act, and many states such as California and Florida require impact statements for certain classes of development. Wherever possible, a local government should try to develop an impact measurement system that is compatible with these other requirements. In general, federal and state requirements are less specific than the detailed measurements suggested in Exhibit 3. Usually the impacts required to be considered are a subset of those in the exhibit. If possible, the various measurement requirements should be translated into a common list of measures that can serve each purpose and avoid redundancy in data collection and analysis.

DATA ANALYSIS: GENERAL ISSUES AND METHODS TO CONSIDER

Some analysis decisions and policies cut across many impact areas. They require the attention of staff directors or persons in charge of development reviews and perhaps even enlightened elected officials. Most of these decisions cannot be abdicated to the various individual analysts of specific types of impacts without losing a coherent review process. Thus, only general analysis issues

are discussed here, in contrast to those related to specific measurement areas, which are treated elsewhere.

Comparison of Development Alternatives

An analysis of development impacts should consider not just what will happen if the proposed development takes place, but what will happen if it does not. Development usually takes place in response to perceived demand. If the demand is not satisfied by the proposed development, it may be met by facilities elsewhere in the community in forms more or less desirable than the proposed one, it may go to other communities, or it may remain unsatisfied. Each of these alternatives implies certain impacts. Most developments have some negative side effects, but not building them may have even worse effects. This is often forgotten in the course of an analysis. For example:

> . . .a no growth policy would not necessarily reduce the need for additional transportation improvements. No growth in Fairfax County could force development into neighboring jurisdictions. . . . (T)rips passing through the county would continue to place demands for further improvements. . .[5]

Where more than one development alternative is proposed or likely to be proposed, these alternatives should be considered, where legally permissible.

Many development proposals include ways to ameliorate potential negative effects of the development, such as landscaping around a parking lot, or a foot-bridge for pedestrians to bypass a road with increased traffic hazard. Unless these are to be legally guaranteed, the development impact should be considered with and without the ameliorating factors.

Choosing the Right Level of Detail for Analysis and Results

Analysis may be conducted at three general levels: qualitative; simple quantitative approximations (sometimes called back-of-the-envelope

---

5. Volume 1, *Presentation of Alternatives,* Five-Year Countywide Development Program, Fairfax County, Virginia (a suburban sector of the Washington, D.C., metropolitan area), 1972.

analysis); and detailed analysis, often with more formalized tools such as computer models and citizen surveys.

The results of the analysis may be presented at corresponding levels of detail—in more general terms, for instance, when there is low confidence in the detailed accuracy of the analysis. To illustrate, results may be described qualitatively: "many people in the neighborhood will be affected"; as a broad range or order of magnitude: "50 to 75 percent of households (hundreds of people) will be affected"; or as detailed estimates: "150 (plus or minus 20) families are likely to be affected."

No rules can be given for selecting the "right" level. In general, unless asked in effect to make the decisions themselves, analysts should probably be encouraged to present results numerically, in terms of end impact. Using numerical ranges is less likely to be misinterpreted than reporting in qualitative terms such as "many," for example. Often information is lost unnecessarily by using qualitative terms.[6]

Sensitivity Analysis

Decision makers should ask that they be told—or check themselves—when the "best estimates" of impacts they are given are very sensitive to the particular assumptions. That is, would slight shifts in the assumptions cause large changes in the impact? Often this information comes out in the course of hearings, but it should not be left to that. Sensitivity analysis, now commonplace in engineering and econometrics, would strengthen land use decision making although it seems to be infrequently employed for this purpose so far. It would help clarify degrees of confidence in estimating impacts.

In projecting development impacts, the uncertainty of the assumptions themselves is often unknown. The accuracy of analytical procedures into which the assumptions are fed may also be uncertain. Therefore it is all the more important to know how much results would vary if initial assumptions varied.

Except when there is high confidence in the

validity of the assumptions behind impact estimates, the analyses should be made for the entire range of plausible assumptions wherever possible. For example, in assessing fiscal impacts there often is considerable uncertainty as to how land use values will change as a result of development—will they go up 10 percent, up 20 percent, or down 10 percent? This uncertainty in turn makes estimates of future revenues from property taxes equally uncertain. The sensitivity of the net fiscal impact to assumptions about property value changes should be considered. That is, if the *most likely* result is an increase of 10 percent, but if a 10 percent drop and a 20 percent rise in land values are also *reasonably possible,* the fiscal impact should be estimated for the range between 20 percent up and 10 percent down (not just for the simple best estimate of 10 percent up.) For another example, when making estimates of changes in air quality there is often uncertainty in the expected per capita usage of automobiles and the expected emissions per car because of uncertainties in such factors as the maintenance of emission control devices, the mix of cars, and the miles driven. The sensitivity of the results to changes in these quantities should be considered.

In general, where initial estimates using single assumptions indicate that there is likely to be a great impact, or at the other extreme indicate virtually no significant impact, sensitivity analyses can often be done in the analyst's head. However, where an initial estimate suggests that an impact may lie near a decision making threshold, or where the analysis indicated great sensitivity of the outcome to particularly narrow or questionable assumptions, then sensitivity analyses should be more formally employed and the results reported.

Undertaking sensitivity analyses should add little cost to the overall analysis since it usually entails a repeated set of computations already thought through. (Of course this is not always so, but checking results for at least one or two additional points than the one thought most likely to occur will not double or triple the cost of the analysis, but will add only a small fraction in most cases.)

Ranges

Ranges for expected impacts should be stated where there is considerable variation possible in

---

6. Note that the numerical quantities suggested here identify end impacts that may be directly comprehended, as opposed to intermediate, technical data that are often hard to interpret.

the estimates. At least the most likely, the high feasible, and low feasible estimates should be given. Of course the range does not imply that every point within it is equally likely. And defining the cut-off for the ranges is a problem itself. But if it is known how much the output varies with the assumptions, one can know how much to be concerned about defining the range of the assumptions.

Long-Term Versus Short-Term Effects

Many impacts of development vary over time. Where possible, impacts should be differentiated by whether their effects will be of short or long duration. For example, construction-related noise, dust, sidewalk and traffic interruptions, and unsightly areas are short-term negative impacts; added jobs from construction are short-term positive impacts.

The ''short term'' in some cases runs into years and the impacts are not insignificant. Construction of the District of Columbia subway, for example, has disrupted some neighborhoods for several years; to avoid disturbing other neighborhoods involved major expenditures to bury at least one station very deeply. Short-term impacts of individual developments also may become long-term impacts when one development triggers another. Thus, so-called short-term effects should not be ignored.

Fiscal impacts is another area where long-term effects are not always appropriately considered. It is often incorrectly assumed, for example, that fiscal flows from a development will be constant (in current dollars) over the long term—ignoring the quality of the building, the changes likely in the neighborhood as housing stock ages and open space declines, and the future residents as well as the immediate ones (in many communities new residents are more affluent, are younger, and have more children in lower grades than the average in the community).

Another class of long-term effects to consider are the foregone or lost opportunities for other types of development and land use if the proposed development is approved. Developing a site today may forego its use for recreation or more appropriate development in the future, for example. Since future voters are not voting today, it is often

much more difficult to take the long-term public interest into account. Nevertheless it should be considered.

When the Proposed Change Is Vague

For many development decisions, especially rezonings other than for PUDs, only the general category of proposed land use may be known, not the specific details of the development. The proposed development then can be almost anything that falls within the uses allowed by the proposed zoning category. For residential development, the zoning category usually at least distinguishes between highrises, garden apartments, and single-family dwellings. For commercial and industrial applications, there are sometimes bounds on the noise level and other environmental impacts. The impact analysis should consider the range of variations in the development possible under the proposed new zoning category, unless the planned use is specified by the developer and likely to be the one that actually gets built—whether by force of law or knowledge of the reliability of the developer. This suggests another reason why sensitivity analyses may be necessary—to explore the range of impacts that may result from the various allowable developments within a revised zoning classification or exception, as well as the variations in other community conditions. Of course the alternative to exploring the range of possibilities within the envelope allowed by the proposed zoning category is to accept the uncertainty about the possible impacts on the community.

Multiple Methods to Improve Confidence

More than one source can sometimes be used to improve confidence in an estimate of a measure.[7] For example, in estimating how citizen satisfaction with neighborhood attractiveness or with recreational opportunity will change as a

---

7. Social scientists sometimes call this ''triangulation.'' You can often improve the ''fix'' on your position (or estimate) by using several different methodologies to make an estimate, where the reliability of each alone is questionable. In advanced navigation or in statistical decision theory, a better estimate can be made using data from several sources, each with known error, than using any single source alone. Unfortunately, the error statistics from social science methodologies often are unknown, and judgments rather than formulas are still needed.

result of development, one might consider combining some of the following approaches: (a) use a scientifically designed citizen survey to establish current perceptions and usage of neighborhood facilities, identifying factors that are liked or disliked; (b) consider the changes that resulted from similar development in comparable neighborhoods and communities; (c) hold public hearings with neighborhood residents, developers, and other interested parties to solicit views on the potential changes from spokesmen and individuals; and (d) hold informal discussions with a small number of residents to understand their concerns in detail.

The accuracy of the information from any of these sources is unknown. Each method has strengths and weaknesses. If all point in the same direction, confidence in the estimated impact would be higher than from using any one.

If the results of using several approaches are mixed, some pointing one way and some another, it is difficult to know which is right. But at least appropriate lines of further inquiry are drawn. For example, if representatives at a public hearing claim the community feels one way, but a citizen survey shows the majority feel another way, one can inquire as to how the representatives obtained their data (from whom, by what process) and can compare this to the results from the random sample broken down by various citizen groupings (for example by area, age, home owner versus renter).

Spatial Scope of Analysis

Development impacts may be localized, communitywide, or spill over into other communities. One cannot safely assume that small developments will not have areawide effects, nor that the localized effects of large developments will be taken care of by constraints imposed by the requested zoning. Usually, individual small developments will have only localized effects, though cumulatively they may have areawide ones. To be on the safe side, possible localized and areawide effects should be considered for all developments.

Secondary Impacts

Frequently a commercial or industrial development will induce later residential develop-

ments to house workers, and may induce demand for additional similar or complementary commercial/industrial development. Often the true impact of the proposed development is the result of a chain of development set in motion, rather than its own, direct impacts. Secondary impacts are frequently ignored, however, in part because they are so difficult to predict or describe quantitatively. Nevertheless, local governments should attempt to consider the chain of impacts that may be triggered by new development. Expression of a range of potential secondary impacts, along with sensitivity analyses would be desirable. At the minimum, they should be described qualitatively.

For example, in reviewing a proposed rezoning of a three-acre, residential parcel for a church, the Indianapolis planning staff noted that:

> If a church is located on too small a site, problems would occur when the church membership grows. Houses surrounding the property would have to be removed to make room for church expansion and church members are forced to park on neighboring streets.[8]

The immediate impact was quite small, but they were careful to consider a potential problem some years in the future.

To Weight or Not to Weight

Most of the impact measurements are incommensurable: there is no ready common denominator for them. Then how do you consider them together? There is a great temptation to create a common denominator by converting each measurement into a number of "points" or into dollar values, and to arrive at a summary "score" for each development. The resulting index (or figure of merit) supposedly expresses the net benefit of the development which can be used for comparing the development against alternative proposals.

Developing a weighting scheme is fraught with problems. Perhaps the biggest one is that there are many value judgments that go into assigning weights and scores, and these judgments are often lost sight of once beyond the hands of

---

8. Indianapolis/Marion County Metropolitan Development Commission Staff Comments, Rezoning Docket of January 14, 1974, 74-Z-10.

the creator of the system. Even though research on the effectiveness of weighting schemes to date suggests that the use of a weighting scheme may lead to more self-consistent decisions, the resultant decisions may not be the right ones.[9] The question is whether individual decision makers should face the problem of different types of impacts having to be considered simultaneously, assigning their own weight to the pros and cons, or allow someone else's judgments or even a consensus judgment to assign the weights to arrive at a "score."

Another problem in using weighting systems is that an impact that may be relatively unimportant most of the time, say on wildlife or informal recreational opportunities, may become extremely important in some development decisions, and may cause a rigid weighting system to be circumvented and thereby discredited. For example, a proposed development in San Francisco was denied for its potential effect on a rare species of flowers that happened to grow at the one spot on the coast where the development was to be built. Although a carefully designed weighting scheme could allow for such dominance by a single factor, the simplistic weighting schemes more likely to be used could cause difficulties.

We recommend that governments rely on human judgment to make the necessary tradeoffs rather than trying to make them mechanistically by a preordained decision scheme,[10] or to use a weighting scheme only as a supplement.

There is an implicit weighting of different types of impacts even when using a measurement system without formal weights. The number of measurements used for a given area may tend to influence its general weight in the overall set of measures. For example, when we divide transportation impacts into distance from mass transit stops, parking availability, travel times, etc., we may be implicitly weighting transportation more heavily than if we just consider one catch-all measure of transportation satisfactoriness. Even the order in which measurement data are presented may bias the implicit weights assigned. Decision makers may get bored part way down the list of measures, and not properly consider items at the end of the list. One way around this is to summarize impacts briefly in an overview table, flagging the most significant measures for the situation at hand, and also summarizing what has and has not been analyzed in depth.

CONSTRAINTS ON USAGE

The experience of this study is that there are some communities and many development situations for which an impact measurement system such as developed in this study can be usefully applied. But there are many barriers—legal, political, organizational, and fiscal—which may make it difficult to fully apply the system in a particular community, or limit its breadth of application.

Legal Constraints

The law varies from state to state and from type of impact to type of impact as to what is allowable. On one hand, the courts have become more broad-minded and allow more considerations than before under the police power or under nuisance law. For example, today there are three states—New York, Oregon, and Florida—which have accepted aesthetics alone as sufficient basis for decisions. At least another four—Louisiana, New Hampshire, Texas, and Wisconsin—have had aesthetics upheld in the courts as the major factor when there are other "minor factors." Another twenty-three states accept aesthetic considerations as a minor factor, one of several reasons for decisions, with the other factors typically being health, safety, or loss of property value. Fourteen more states and the District of Columbia allow the vague consideration of "character of the district," which may include aesthetics. The remaining seven states apparently have no specific references one way or the other.[11]

9. An excellent discussion of formal approaches for making decisions using incommensurable data may be found in Douglas C. Dacy, et al., *Approaches to the Treatment of Incommensurables in Cost-Benefit Analyses*, prepared for the National Science Foundation by the Institute for Defense Analysis, Arlington, Virginia, 1973.

10. A similar conclusion for similar reasons is reached in Oglesby, et al., *Highway Research Record No. 305*, Highway Research Board, Washington, D.C., 1970, p.3.

11. Dennis Minano, "Aesthetic Zoning: The Creation of a New Standard," *Journal of Urban Law*, Vol. 48, No. 3, April 1971. Many useful references on the status of aesthetics in the law may be found in James W. Cerney, "Aesthetics and Jurisprudence: A Bibliographic Primer," Exchange Bibliography No. 408, Council of Planning Librarians, Monticello, Illinois, 1973.

The law has changed from the early 1900s position stated by the New Jersey Court, that:

> Aesthetic considerations are a matter of luxury and indulgence rather than necessity, and it is necessity alone which justifies the exercise of the police power to take private property without compensation. . .

to the position stated by Justice William Douglas in 1954 in a U.S. Supreme Court ruling which said:

> It is within the power of the legislature to determine that the community should be beautiful as well as healthy, spacious as well as clean, well balanced as well as carefully patrolled. . .If those who govern the District of Columbia decide that the nation's capital should be beautiful as well as sanitary, there is nothing in the Fifth Amendment that stands in the way. . .[12]

On the other hand, most courts continue to take a hard look at the basis for rejecting proposed development, and many local governments—perhaps most—have had their decisions successfully challenged.

It is sometimes forgotten that the standards or threshold values set by state and federal governments often incorporate safety factors whose magnitude is based primarily on human judgment as to how large a margin is needed, and not on clear evidence. The courts seem to be recognizing that some "soft" analytical areas are important, and that some areas thought to have "hard" data may not be as solid as they seem on the surface. Since most laws do not specifically indicate which types of impacts may be considered, local governments will have to identify their allowable range from recent court decisions or by new court tests. For example, in Montgomery County, Maryland, a court test may be pending to clarify the implications of the new "adequate public facilities" ordinance, to determine what public facilities are included, and what is the definition of "adequate."

The courts generally encourage use of "standards" in local government decision making, to help ensure consistency and thereby fairness. The consistent use of a measurement checklist may help a local government demonstrate consistency of its evaluation approach. But it also, by the very same argument, could require developments to be evaluated at the same level of detail in each analysis. That is, if in reviewing one development it seemed appropriate to do a detailed localized air pollution assessment, it is conceivable that the local government could be required to do a detailed analysis on all or no developments. In other words, the use of the measurement system with discretion as to the level of detail needed for analyzing particular measures may be seen as not much more consistent treatment than an ad hoc procedure. How this will turn out remains to be seen.[13]

As mentioned earlier, some types of development decisions allow much more discretion to the local government than others: PUDs are the classic case in point; there the local government often has a great deal of discretion over the details of site planning. Local governments also increasingly are using bonus systems for developers, whereby minimum requirements for developments are waived in return for obtaining other public benefits. One of the most common types of trading arrangements is to allow a developer to build more intensely—more square feet or building height than is normally allowed for the site—in return for providing public amenities such as plazas or shopping arcades. These horse trading arrangements may include types of impacts not normally allowed to be considered directly.

It is no secret that local governments can apply great leverage to developers by nitpicking enforcement of laws and codes. Also, legally defensible criteria such as sewer capacities may be used as an excuse when other impacts are really dominant in the decision. Thus many criteria get considered even if not officially condoned.

Political Constraints

It is pointless to spend resources developing new or more detailed information if it will not get a fair hearing. Where the decision making body is dominated by no growth interests, where citizens

---

12. William H. Agnor, "Beauty Begins a Comeback: Aesthetic Considerations in Zoning," *Journal of Public Law,* Vol. 11, 1962, pp. 261-284. Agnor gives the exact citations for these and many other related cases.

13. For a more detailed discussion on the legal framework behind impact measures, see Michael Mandel, "The Various Legal Frameworks for Utilizing Impact Measures in Land Use Decision Making," Working Paper, The Urban Institute, 1975.

would like to pull up the drawbridge, it may be difficult to get a development approved unless shown to have extremely good benefits for the community. At the other extreme, decision making may be dominated by interests which feel that all development should be allowed unless demonstrated to have very negative impacts on the community—that is, a generally laissez faire attitude exists. In these cases, the decision process becomes less a matter of evaluating pros and cons than an adversary situation, often between planning staff and decision makers. It may be futile in these situations to develop an impact measurement system. On the other hand, political considerations sometimes may be dominant *because* of the lack of persuasive evidence that the development impacts can be forecast accurately enough to decide the issues primarily on their merits. This is not to say that political judgments would not have to be made if the impacts were entirely predictable—they would; but the facts of each case would play a greater role in those judgments. Finally, political decision makers will often rely on staff judgments if for no other reason than the lack of time for officials to analyze each case, leaving the way open for the planning staff to use comprehensive impact analyses.

An aware and participating citizenry can be a major aid to land use planning. Yet, if citizens get the impression that the measurement system gives the planning staff answers which in fact are beyond the state of the art or that would be too expensive to answer for every development, public demands for the measurement information may bog down the decision making process so much that the staff may feel it is better not to have a set of measures in explicit, formal use.

Where citizens are not especially active, impact measurements—especially those involving use of citizen surveys—are sometimes viewed negatively as having the potential to "stir up" neighborhoods against development that may be desirable.

Another type of political constraint comes from the weight often given to the opinions of those citizens who attend hearings. The degree to which they represent their community usually is not adequately identified. They may be viewed as representing a bloc of votes or as typifying concerned citizens who should be given primary

attention. Citizen views expressed at hearings are unquestionably important. But if they are given undue weight, planning staff may be less likely to undertake other forms of analysis such as citizen surveys which may yield different or more balanced views.

The development community may be expected at least initially to be concerned about the implementation of an impact measurement system. They are likely to view it, often rightly so, as creating the possibility of additional delays in decision making while staff analysis takes place, complicating the decision with more considerations, each of which may be challenged, and possibly requiring them to provide additional data too. The result may be slightly increased cost to consumer to make up for the increased costs to the developer in idle investment and additional workload. What is hard to show is whether the consumers gain anything, at least in the long run, from presumably improved decision information. One recent study has shown that the evaluation process for "developments or regional impact" in Florida adds up to about $100 per housing unit. Thus there often is an explicit cost but an implicit benefit. What developers can hope to gain is a fairer decision by making the process more consistent from one time to another, and in the longer run a better community in which to operate. If this is not so, then the measurement should not be used.

There is yet another type of problem that might be considered political or institutional: the capabilities of the decision makers. Land use decisions commonly involve part-time officials, often the zoning commission. The members frequently are political appointees who donate time to serve. They often cannot spend much time reviewing individual developments. Although measurement systems can help reduce the problem by using a common language that makes problem identification easier to spot from case to case, the members may prefer only to be told the one or two key issues and not the subsidiary ones which collectively may be important.

The ability to understand the results of analysis is another related problem. The use of measures will fall flat unless the users have some "number sense." Although a skillful staff can translate the results of an analysis based on measures for the decision makers, the measurement system itself may not be usable directly in presentation to decision makers due to either their time or training limitations.

In summary, unless there is a possibility for at least reasonably objective review and openmindedness by decision makers and citizens on the issues, there may not be much point in developing improved information.

Technological Constraints

There are many impacts that most would agree should be estimated for development if a practical way could be found to do so. Estimates of citizen satisfaction with various services and their community may fall into this category. Measures for which no practical methodology exists for data collection and analysis cannot be used except perhaps in qualitative modes. When a large enough number of measures are beyond the state of the art or beyond the means of the local government, one may question the utility of a measurement system. However, we suggest that regardless of the level of technical sophistication and resources in a local government, a systematic approach to assessing impacts—even if it is largely qualitative—may be superior to ad hoc qualitative estimations. This was the consensus of most members of our Advisory Group, though some felt that a measurement cannot be used unless it can be reliably estimated quantitatively and supported in court.

Organizational Constraints

A planning staff may resist a new measurement system because of fears that its use will lock them into a heavier workload. They may have the misimpression that they will have to supply data for each measure for every development, or for significantly more developments than they do now. While some increase is possible, it should be kept in mind that the system may be used in many modes, and detailed analyses will be necessary only on a very selective basis.

Obviously, the resources available for development review and planning—money, staff time, calendar time, staff skills—limit the number

and depth of analyses that can be conducted. However, just because the list of measures is long and there are a large number of developments proposed each year does not make the system unworkable. As noted earlier, only a few measures, if any, are likely to be significant for most small and even medium-size developments. Much of the analysis can be qualitative and pro forma. Usually only a few of the larger or more precedent-setting developments will require extensive analysis, and they already receive lengthy analysis, whatever evaluation approach is taken.

Cost Constraints

Unfortunately, we do not have a good estimate of the cost of typical analyses because of the difficulty of assessing incremental changes from current procedures and because of the wide range of analysis possibilities from superficial to highly detailed. Much of the increased expense in undertaking impact analysis is likely to come from one-time set-up costs to obtain computer models and get them working (for assessing air or water quality, for example). Of course, these same costs may be incurred whether or not the impact measurement system is adopted. Other one-time costs are associated with developing citizen surveys or obtaining baseline data, though these surveys might be repeated once a year. An overall citizen survey might cost $10,000 to $20,000 for a large community, with approximately 100 families sampled in each of five to ten districts. Surveys confined to those areas of a community that are most likely to undergo further development could reduce this cost. Mini-surveys to supplement information from the overall baseline survey and to get more detailed information on small areas undergoing development could add to the cost.

Although costs are unclear, a system of measurements can be adapted to virtually any size planning and review budget. The system can be beneficial even if used only qualitatively, as mentioned earlier. Also, many developments are routine repetitions of similar ones that have occurred before in the community. The prototype analysis for such classes of developments can probably be used over and over, with minor modifications to adjust for the small localized variations likely to occur.

VII. EXAMPLES OF DEVELOPMENT REVIEWS USING IMPACT CHECKLIST

Some initial tests have been conducted with a comprehensive impact measurement system of the kind discussed in the preceding chapters. The tests involved actual developments, but to avoid having the experiment disrupt the actual and time-critical process, the results were not applied to the decision making process. A full-scale test of the use of an impact measurement system was not possible during the study which provided the basis for this report.

Three types of applications of an impact measurement checklist are cited: (1) for qualitative, quick analysis of two small proposed rezonings; (2) for evaluating zoning adjustments; and (3) for attempting a detailed analysis of a large proposed planned development. The three communities that undertook the testing—Indianapolis, Indiana; Phoenix, Arizona; and Montgomery County, Maryland—are quite different from one another. A summary of the participants' own assessments of using the measurement system is discussed in Chapter IX.

QUICK, QUALITATIVE ANALYSES

A measurement checklist adapted from that in Exhibit 3 was used by planning staff members in Indianapolis, Indiana to briefly review two small proposed rezonings. The reviews were based on knowledge of existing conditions at the site and the specific uses that were proposed. They are highly judgmental.

These two examples illustrate several points. First, many impact areas can be quickly dismissed as not pertinent. Only a relatively small number seem significant and less than a handful appeared as key ones in any given analysis. Second, the lack of data stands in the way of judging significance, even qualitatively, for some types of impacts. This checklist approach, however, at least identified the omissions explicitly. Third, various impacts that were not considered during the actual ad hoc type of review were identified by using the comprehensive list.[1]

Example 1: Small Proposed Rezoning in Indianapolis

The proposed rezoning was for a small parcel of land from light industrial to heavy industrial. The site was adjacent to an old residential neighborhood. The site was not actively in use and contained only the foundation of an old railroad roadhouse. The expected new use was an automobile shredding operation—converting junk cars to scrap.

---

1. The impact data presented here were not validated and therefore their accuracy is not known. The use of an impact measurement system may indirectly help improve accuracy of estimates over the long run by helping to identify the best data collection procedures, using the same ones repeatedly and making them known: data often improves over time when it is used in substantive decisions. But accuracy of methodology can certainly be improved independent of a measurement system.

The results of the analysis are summarized in Exhibit 7. All measures were briefly scanned to see if they were likely to be relevant, that is, suggesting a significant impact.

This development seemed, in summary, to offer significant benefits to the owners and oprators of the new plant, a likely fiscal "profit" for the community as a whole, and a place for a useful service that has wide community aesthetic benefits. On the deficit side, considerable noise and air quality (dust) problems were highly likely to be raised for nearby residents. In fact, the development was approved and built, and led to considerable citizen protest over the airborne particulate matter that resulted.

Applying the measurement checklist helped to identify several positive and negative impacts which had not been explicitly considered in the original ad hoc evaluation. These included fiscal impacts, and changes in air quality, loss of landmarks, and crime hazard. (Potential impacts in several other measurement areas also had not been considered but were evaluated as having negligible potential impacts.) However, it was felt by the planning staff that the decision probably would not have changed with the additional information, though the systematic approach did highlight the severe air quality impact and might have prepared officials for the reaction to this feature, even if the decision did not change.

EXHIBIT 7
QUALITATIVE EVALUATION OF PROPOSED INDUSTRIAL REZONING IN INDIANAPOLIS

MEASURE NUMBER[a]	IMPACT AREA AND MEASURE	DEGREE OF EXPECTED IMPACT ON:[b]		EXPECTED IMPACT AND ANALYSIS SUMMARY[c]
		Neighborhood	Community at Large	
	Local Economy			
1.	Public fiscal flows	0	+	Tax revenues expected to be considerably larger than cost of public services. Site expected to remain vacant (with low taxes) unless rezoned, because light industry for which site was zoned has moved to suburban areas. Proposed new use seemed to require little in way of added public service expense. (However, possible loss in revenues from decrease in residential property value in vicinity may affect net gain somewhat.)
2-3.	Employment	0	+	Few new jobs; no old ones displaced.
4.	Property values	−	?	Expected increase in value of site falling to new owner; possible decrease in value of nearby homes because of nuisance added. (On the other hand, prices of residential property might rise because of speculation on their potential for being rezoned industrial.)

Using An Impact Measurement System

EXHIBIT 7 (CONT.)

MEASURE NUMBER[a]	IMPACT AREA AND MEASURE	DEGREE OF EXPECTED IMPACT ON:[b]		EXPECTED IMPACT AND ANALYSIS SUMMARY[c]
		Neighborhood	Community at Large	
	Natural Environment			
5.	Air quality	— —	–	Frequent trucks to and from site expected to raise clouds of dust, affecting people in adjacent neighborhood and possibly beyond.
6.	Water quality (bodies of water)	0	0	No apparent effect (See 18, however).
7.	Noise and vibration levels	— —	0	Nearby houses affected by noise from automobile shredding machine (and increase in truck traffic?).
8.	Greenery and open space	0	0	No expected increase in landscaping; none there at present. (Open space decreased somewhat.)
9-10.	(Measure deleted in Indianapolis)			
11.	Energy consumption	0	0	Shredder is intensive user of electrical energy but not likely to affect supply by itself. Not unusual usage relative to process, though high relative to auto junkyard.
12.	Natural disasters— flooding	0	0	No effect.
	Aesthetics and Cultural Values			
13.	Views degraded or blocked			Adjacent neighborhood views and pedestrian views blocked by 35-foot high pile of scrap and 8-12 foot fence.
14.	Attractiveness and architectural compatibility	— —	+	Planned structure, fence, and junk pile will significantly worsen neighborhood attractiveness (though existing attractiveness was not very great). However, attractiveness of other parts of the community may be improved by removing abandoned cars from dumps or even streets, where they stay in view instead of being shredded.
15.	(Measure deleted)			
16.	Landmarks	–	–	Old railroad roundhouse to be destroyed; neighborhood landmark, city landmark (though not a visitors' attraction).

EXHIBIT 7 (CONT.)

MEASURE NUMBER[a]	IMPACT AREA AND MEASURE	DEGREE OF EXPECTED IMPACT ON:[b]		EXPECTED IMPACT AND ANALYSIS SUMMARY[c]
		Neighborhood	Community at Large	
	Public and Private Services			
17.	Drinking water— shortages	0	0	No effect.
18.	Drinking water— safety	?	0	Possible subsurface pollution (needs further review to see if nearby houses use wells).
19-20.	Hospital services	0	0	No effect.
21-22.	Crime control	—	0	Fences to be added around (now) open site will block sightlines, add hiding places for attackers and possibly increase neighborhood crime or feelings of insecurity somewhat.
23-24.	Fire protection	?	0	Probably little impact, though piles of materials such as tires may add risk of tempting incendiarism. (No new public fire equipment needed, no major affect on neighborhood fire risk.)
25-26.	Recreation— accessibility, usage	0	0	Children did not seem to play on the unused lot (based on observations) before, so no immediate effect.
27.	Recreation—perceived pleasantness	?	0	No effect unless children used nearby streets for informal recreation, which could be made unpleasant by increase in dust and noise. (See 5, 7 above.)
28.	Education—accessibility	0	0	Path through the lot, used as a safe shortcut by neighborhood children walking to school, would increase children's walk by 1-2 blocks, except that developer agreed to put sidewalk through his property for use by children.
29-30.	Education—bus crowdedness	0	0	No impact.
31-36.	Transportation	0	0	No significant impact; nearby railroad brings junk cars to the site; truck traffic increase (for hauling away scrap) should not increase local travel times or congestion much, nor affect nearby public transportation or parking.
37-38.	Shopping	0	0	No impact.

EXHIBIT 7 (CONT.)

MEASURE NUMBER[a]	IMPACT AREA AND MEASURE	DEGREE OF EXPECTED IMPACT ON:[b]		EXPECTED IMPACT AND ANALYSIS SUMMARY[c]
		Neighborhood	Community at Large	
	Housing and Social Conditions			
39-40.	Housing supply	0 (?)	0 (?)	No apparent impact (unless environment of adjacent housing becomes so undesirable as to make them unusable, or unless the rezoning leads to other rezoning of nearby residential properties and their replacement by industry).
41.	People displaced	0	0	None.
42.	Population mix	0	0	No change expected.
43.	Perceived crowdedness	0	0	No change expected.
44-45.	Sociability/Friendliness	0	0	No change expected (site is on fringe of neighborhood; no interference with paths between neighborhood residents).
46-47.	Privacy	0	0	No significant change expected (some sightlines removed, but none affecting privacy much).
48.	Overall neighborhood satisfaction	− or ——	0	Probably would significantly decrease satisfaction of at least those residents within earshot of the noise to be added or near the dust raised.
Other	Hazard to children: degree of "attractive nuisance"	−	0	The junkyard will probably attract children to "play" there; they may get injured amid the debris.

a. The numbered measures correspond to those in Schaenman and Muller, *Measuring Impacts on Land Development,* op. cit., Exhibit 1, pp. 10-11. They are quite similar to the ones in Exhibit 3 of this report. The only areas dropped from the measurement list were wildlife and citizen rating of attractiveness.

b. The symbols used are as follows: ++ Very positive (beneficial) impact
+ Somewhat positive impact
0 Apparently neutral or no impact
− Somewhat negative (detrimental) impact
—— Very negative impact
? Considerable uncertainty about net impact

c. Comments are by Indianapolis staff (except for comments in parentheses, by the author).

An evaluation of this type could be improved by developing at least rough quantitative approximations of the impacts thought to be significant. For example, how far would noise from the trucks reach at annoying decibel levels, and what numbers of people would be affected? What was the current usage of the outdoor areas where environments would be affected (by noise and dust) for informal recreation? How large a "profit" would be yielded in taxes over public expenditures, in the short-run and long-run? Decision makers would thus be alerted to vital issues.

Example 2: Another Small Proposed Rezoning in Indianapolis

The proposed rezoning was for a small tract from "medium industrial suburban" district to "commercial-industrial" district. The requested new uses were a truck stop, motel, and restaurant. Allowed under the existing zoning were food processing plants, manufacturing; power plants; and motor truck terminals less than ten acres in total area. The site was vacant, however.

Considering the summary of impacts shown in Exhibit 8, this may appear at first to be a strange case. There are no apparent benefits and no special detriments indicated (though the analysts felt that fiscal and employment impacts could not be estimated).

Let us assume that this analysis was, in fact, complete, with the same results—no apparent positive or negative impacts. What does this mean? Probably that the benefits and detriments to the community are too diffuse to detect, not that they do not exist. The most direct benefit is to the owners of the proposed business, and their customers (in this case, mostly transients). If the land was not previously developed, there probably would be a net gain in public fiscal revenues over fiscal expenses and a slight gain in employment, but only if the business was new to the community or displaced a small or less successful one elsewhere in the community. There are also likely to be minor degradations in environment and minor contributions to the economy as a whole.

The impact analysis here serves to screen out any major problems. In-depth analysis of such a

---

EXHIBIT 8
ANOTHER BRIEF QUALITATIVE IMPACT EVALUATION OF AN INDUSTRIAL REZONING IN INDIANAPOLIS

MEASURE NUMBER[a]	IMPACT AREA AND MEASURES	DEGREE OF EXPECTED IMPACT ON:[b]		EXPECTED IMPACT AND ANALYSIS SUMMARY[c]
		Neighborhood	Community at Large	
	Local Economy			
1.	Public fiscal flows	?	?	Could not estimate.
2-3.	Employment	?	?	Could not estimate.
4.	Property values	0	0	Minimal change expected because area was already zoned industrial, though for somewhat different types of industries.
	Natural Environment			
5.	Air quality	–	0	Possible increase in air pollutants in vicinity of development due to large number of trucks expected.
6.	Water quality	0	0	Insignificant.
7.	Noise and vibration levels	–	0	Significant increase in neighborhood of development.
8.	Greenery and open space	?	0	Cannot estimate; no site plan available.
9-10.	Deleted	n/a	n/a	
11.	Energy consumption	0	0	No significant impact.

Using An Impact Measurement System

EXHIBIT 8 (CONT.)

MEASURE NUMBER[a]	IMPACT AREA AND MEASURES	DEGREE OF EXPECTED IMPACT ON:[b]		EXPECTED IMPACT AND ANALYSIS SUMMARY[c]
		Neighborhood	Community at Large	
12.	Natural disasters	0	0	No apparent hazard.
	Aesthetics and cultural values			
13.	Views	0	0	No apparent effect.
14.	Visual attractiveness and architectural compatibility	?	?	No renderings available.
15.	Deleted by Indianapolis (citizen rating of attractiveness)	n/a	n/a	
16.	Landmarks	0	0	Not affected.
	Public & Private Services			
17-18.	Drinking water	0	0	Not affected.
19-20.	Hospital care	0	0	Not affected.
21-22.	Crime control	0	0	Insignificant effects.
23-24.	Fire protection	0	0	No significant effect.
25-27.	Recreation	0	0	Not affected.
28-30.	Education	0	0	Not affected.
31-34.	Transportation—travel time, congestion, parking, and access to public transit	0	0	No significant effect.
35.	Transportation—hazards	0	0	No effect if necessary local traffic controls needed for increased traffic pulling in and out of site are added.
36.	Transportation—pedestrian usage and hazard	0	0	No effect.
37-38.	Shopping	0	0	Not affected.
39-48.	*Housing and Social Conditions*	0	0	No apparent effects.

a. The numbered measures correspond to those in Schaenman and Muller, *Measuring Impacts on Land Development*, op. cit., Exhibit 1, pp. 10-11.

b. The symbols used are as follows: ++ Very positive (beneficial) impact
  + Somewhat positive impact
  0 Apparently neutral or no impact
  – Somewhat negative (detrimental) impact
  –– Very negative impact
  ? Considerable uncertainty about net impact

c. Comments are by Indianapolis staff.

situation is rarely justified. The impacts of such types of development probably are best considered cumulatively as a part of the planning process. But at least a quick check on major positive and negative impacts, including localized ones not likely to be identified in planning, should be undertaken.

Example 3: Evaluating a Series of Zoning Adjustments in Phoenix

In Phoenix, the Zoning Administrator has responsibility for deciding on certain zoning adjustments such as variances and changes in land use requiring use permits.[2] Exhibit 9 shows a typical agenda of cases. The agenda was annotated by the Zoning Administrator to reflect those impact areas requiring special attention in each case.

The checklist is used very informally in this application—mainly as an aide-memoire. The administrator makes field inspections for each use

---

2. The decisions may be appealed to the Board of Adjustment and then to the court.

change. Virtually all cases are decided on qualitative considerations. The degree of impact is judgmentally determined, with a modest amount of research on the changes. Since the hearing involves the staff/decision-maker as one party directly dealing with the applicant or his representative (and possibly other interested parties), there usually is no need to quantitatively estimate impacts or to document them formally. The administrator himself can usually visualize the number of persons whose views may be affected and weigh this against the added jobs, for example, or the new shopping and service opportunity provided by the proposed new use.

Note that even in the short, one-day agenda used as illustration in Exhibit 9, economic, aesthetic, natural environment, public service, and social impacts arise. Note also the preponderance of social impacts—those often considered "soft" and difficult to deal with in rezonings and in the courts; it is not too surprising that these considerations are central to what goes on in people's backyards.

EXHIBIT 9
INFORMAL, QUALITATIVE IMPACT CONSIDERATIONS IDENTIFIED FOR A SERIES OF ZONING ADJUSTMENTS
City of Phoenix, Arizona, Planning Department
Calendar of cases for consideration by the Zoning Administrator on July 1, 1975.

CALENDAR ITEM	CASE NUMBER, SUBJECT, PERTINENT LAW, AND ZONING CATEGORY	MAIN IMPACT ISSUES [a]
1.	427-75 USE PERMIT requested for sale of alcoholic beverages as accessory use to restaurant. (#16 License). Use Permit required. Sec. 416 c. Commercial C-1	Employment Noise Parking-Traffic Neighborhood
2.	428-75 VARIANCES requested to: (1) Delete a portion of wall bordering parking area; (2) Delete a portion of safety curbing. (1) 3' solid wall required. (2) Must be curbed except for ingress and egress. Sec. 601 B, 5; 601 B, 8. Residence R1-6	Aesthetics Parking-Traffic Neighborhood
3.	429-75 VARIANCE requested to build swimming pool in front yard. Shall be in side or rear yard. Sec. 506 B. Residence R1-10	Attractiveness Privacy

EXHIBIT 9 (CONT.)

CALENDAR ITEM	CASE NUMBER, SUBJECT, PERTINENT LAW, AND ZONING CATEGORY	MAIN IMPACT ISSUES[a]
4.	430-75 VARIANCE requested for 6' wood fence with approximately 5' setback from street side property line of corner lot contiguous to key lot. 10' minimum setback required. Sec. 503 C. Residence R-5	Views Attractiveness Traffic hazard Land values
5.	431-75 VARIANCE requested to build addition to house with approximately 17' rear yard setback (from alley center line). 25' minimum required. Sec. 408 B, 4. Residence R1-6	Attractiveness Crowdedness Land Values
6.	432-75 USE PERMIT requested to change from one nonconforming use (tavern) to another nonconforming use (toy and antique store) upon sale. Use Permit required. Sec. 110 E Residence R-5	Land values Noise Parking-Traffic Neighborhood
7.	433-75 (1) USE PERMIT requested for medical-dental laboratories in C-O zone; (2) VARIANCE requested to provide entrance to laboratory from other than within exterior walls of building. (1) Use Permit required. (2) Must be from within exterior walls of building. Sec. 411.1 A,4,b. Commercial C-0 (Lab for use of patients on-premises.)	Transportation Employment Land values Medical care Neighborhood
8.	434-75 VARIANCE requested to use mobile home for living purposes on lot not in mobile home development (while building home). Must be in mobile home development. Sec. 400 K. Residence R1-14	Neighborhood Land values Crime control Crowdedness
9.	Withdrawn	
10.	436-75 VARIANCE requested to use mobile home for living purposes (caretaker) on lot not in mobile home development. Must be in mobile home development. Sec. 400 K. Suburban S-2	Crime control Land values Neighborhoods
11.	437-75 APPEAL Zoning Inspector's decision that storage and repair of clothing, furniture, toys, etc., and storage of food for distribution to needy is not accessory use to church. Chapt. II — Def. (Accessory Use). Residence R-4	Neighborhood Traffic-Parking Sociability Population Mix
12.	438-75 VARIANCE requested to build stairway in P-1 zone. No structures except carports permitted. Sec. 422A. Parking P-1 & Commercial (Stairway in government office building to accommodate handicapped persons.)	Aesthetics Parking Population Mix Health service

a. Noted by Zoning Administrator.

Examples of Development Reviews

Example 4: Quantitative Analysis of a Planned Unit Development in Montgomery County, Maryland

The proposed development for a 76-acre site consisted of: a mixture of townhouses, garden apartments, and "elevator gardens" (about 10 percent intended for moderate-income families); local commercial space; property dedicated to the county for a high school and an elementary school. The remainder of the tract was left as open green space, part for community use. (The tract was mostly open green space, privately owned, prior to the proposed development.)

Exhibit 10 shows the results of an impact analysis of the proposal. Except for a few minor editorial changes, the exhibit is as prepared by the Montgomery County planning staff. Impacts are stated separately for (a) the "planning area"—a significant part of the county used as the basic unit for planning; (b) the neighborhood of the development, and (c) for some measures, a further breakdown between the site itself ("W/L" for Wall-Luttrell planned development) and the rest of the neighborhood. The exhibit also shows the extent to which the development complies with existing comprehensive plans.

The measures and format in Exhibit 10 are those from Exhibits 1 and 4, Schaenman and Muller.[3] (A slightly revised set of measures is given

in Exhibit 3 of this report.) For some measures, such as 5 and 6, both a qualitative estimate of the preferred measure and the quantitative intermediate measures on which it is based were given. In some cases, a variation on the suggested measure was used.

Most of the data presented were not collected specifically for this study, but rather were extracted from various sources (such as the developer's proposal and planning staff comments) that had been developed by the county's own review of this proposal. The measurement system recasts the data into a condensed form showing what was considered and where some types of data were lacking. It emphasizes end impacts (e.g., change in air quality) rather than harder to interpret technical data (e.g., percentage change in vehicle emissions). Certain social impacts (Measures 43–47) were not considered as part of the original analysis and could not be analyzed in retrospect.

Perhaps the most interesting aspect of this example is the extent of detailed, comprehensive data that was amassed in the course of the project review via an "organic"/preplanned tools approach rather than the measurement checklist approach. Although not illustrated here, there was also a series of back-up reports, showing further details of the significant impacts and how each impact was determined—whether by pure judgment, computer models, citizen surveys, citizen hearings, and so forth. The source may make a significant difference in the weight a decision maker attaches to an outcome.

---

3. Schaenman and Muller, op. cit.

EXHIBIT 10

EVALUATION OF A PROPOSED PLANNED UNIT DEVELOPMENT
The Wall-Luttrell Planned Development, Montgomery County, Maryland[1]

IMPACT AREA	MEASURE	IMPACT ON CLIENTELE GROUPS		COMPLIANCE WITH COMPREHENSIVE PLANS
		Planning Area	Neighborhood—Including Low and Moderate Income Families	
I. Local Economy Public fiscal balance	1. Net change in government fiscal flow.	+ $300,000 to $400,000.	n/a[2]	n/a—Plan not based on fiscal flows.
Employment	2. Number of new long-term and short-term jobs provided.	+200 jobs (mostly short-term, associated with construction of development).	n/a	Yes.
	3. Change in numbers and percent employed, unemployed, and underemployed.	No change (not possible to measure).	n/a	Yes.
Wealth	4. Change in property values.	+$2-5 million.	n/a	Yes.
II. Natural Environment Air	5. Change in level of air pollutants and number of people at risk or bothered by air pollution.	No change in air quality. 1-3% increase in vehicle emissions. 2-5% increase in household emissions.	Negligible change in ambient air quality. 7% increase in vehicle emissions (CO, HC, NO_x). 19% increase in household emissions (CO, NO_x, particulates, and SO_2).	Yes.
Water	6. Change in level of water pollutants, change in tolerable types of use, and number of persons affected—by each body of water.	Significant degradation in quality of stream running through site; no impacts for other bodies of water. 5.9% increase in sewage flow from the planning area to be treated at public plants.	18.9% increase in sewage flow from the neighborhood to be treated at public plants. Storm water runoff will increase 48% from this site.	Master Plan allows for sewage flows, but there may be trunk sewer transmission constraint. A Comprehensive Storm Water Management Plan is now being prepared.

EXHIBIT 10 (CONT.)

| IMPACT AREA | MEASURE | IMPACT ON CLIENTELE GROUPS | | COMPLIANCE WITH COMPREHENSIVE PLANS |
		Planning Area	Neighborhood—Including Low and Moderate Income Families	
Noise	7. Change in noise and vibration levels, and number of people bothered by excessive noise and vibration.	Barely detectable to a trained observer. Increase of 1 DBA (decibel).3	Minor impact. Increase of 5 DBA on adjacent property. Several units along Old Georgetown Road could slightly exceed HUD standards. Units along Wall Lane will exceed HUD standards when windows are open.	No master plan for noise factors.
Greenery and open space	8. Amount and percent change in greenery and open space—on the development itself and in the community.	(Did not compute areas of green space in the planning area.)	Negligible. Computed a 3% loss in total neighborhood green space; 12% loss in continuous neighborhood open space (park land, large private parcels, etc.).	Yes.
Wildlife and vegetation	9. Number and types of endangered or rare species that will be threatened.	None known.	None known.	n/a
	10. Change in abundance and diversity of wildlife.	None known.	Squirrels will temporarily decrease in number. When project is complete, bird population will likely be larger than before followed by a slow return of squirrels in 2-4 years. Bird types will tend toward foragers; e.g., sparrow, wrens, etc.	n/a

Scarce resource consumption	11. Change in frequency, duration and magnitude of shortages, and the number of persons affected.	n/a	A temporary shortage of fuel oil or natural gas could occur if the houses use gas or oil heat. Low-income families would likely be more severely affected due to an inability to pay premium prices or convert to a different system.	No.
Natural Disasters	12. Change in number of people and value of property endangered by flooding, earthquakes, land slides, mud slides, and other natural disasters.	None known.	A 100-year storm (e.g., Agnes) could flood the bottom floors of several apartments along Edson Lane despite the storm water management devices. Low-income housing is generally located away from stream park land and would be protected.	Yes.
III. Aesthetics and Cultural Values Views	13. Number of people whose views are blocked; degraded; or improved.	n/a	None—A 100 foot buffer between development and the Luxmanor Development screens the new development.	Yes. PD-9 (Planned Development) is proposed for this property.
Attractiveness	14. Visual attractiveness of the development as rated by citizens and "experts."	n/a n/a	Good—Citizens endorsed the site plan. During hearing, attractiveness a factor. Experts: Good.	n/a
	15. Percent of citizens who think the development improves or lessens the overall neighborhood attractiveness, pleasantness, and uniqueness.	This application is probably more attractive than R-90 which is allowed by right. Also citizens, through government officials, have more influence over the physical attractiveness of this development because of site plan review.		Yes—PD-9 is proposed for this property.
Landmarks	16. Rarity and perceived importance of cultural, historic, or scientific landmarks to be lost or made inaccessible.	The Luttrell house will be maintained as a community center, making it more accessible to neighborhood and planning area residents than previously.		Subject is not mentioned in master plan.

EXHIBIT 10 (CONT.)

IMPACT AREA	MEASURE	IMPACT ON CLIENTELE GROUPS		COMPLIANCE WITH COMPREHENSIVE PLANS
		Planning Area	Neighborhood—Including Low and Moderate Income Families	
IV. Public and Private Services Drinking water	17. Change in rate of water shortage incidents.	Minimal. 166,000 gallons/day used by development. 129,000,000 gallons/day used by service area = .10%. This project should have no problems, since it is on public water supply.	Minimal.	Yes.
	18. Change in indexes of drinking water quality and safety.	No change.	No change.	n/a
Hospital care	19. Change in number and percent of citizens who are beyond x minutes travel time from a hospital emergency room.	No change.	n/a	Yes.
	20. Change in average number of days of waiting time for hospital admittance for elective surgery.	No change.	n/a	Yes.
Crime control	21. Change in rate of crimes—by whether against existing community or new development.	Cannot evaluate.	Same.	n/a
	22. Change in percent of people feeling a lack of security from crime.	Cannot evaluate.	Same.	n/a
Fire protection	23. Change in fire incidence rates.	+ 6.8 fires based on current incidence rates.	Same.	Yes.
	24. Change in rating of fire spread and rescue hazards.	No significant change.	Same.	Yes.

Recreation			
25. Change in the number of people within—or beyond—a reasonable distance from recreational facilities—by type of facility.	Because the developer is supplying an excess of recreation facilities and open space, the existing facilities in the planning area should be less crowded as residents from other areas will use some of the facilities in Wall-Luttrell.	Number of facilities supplied are in excess or equal to those normally provided by the Public Park Program. These facilities and park land are at most ¼ mile from each resident in the development:	Yes—although recreational facilities distributed throughout community rather than consolidated into park portion of park school.
26. Change in usage as a percent of capacity; waiting time, number of people turned away; facility space per resident; and citizen perceptions of crowdedness at recreational facilities.	n/a	1 swimming pool per 1,000 people. 1 tennis court per 500 people. 1 multi-purpose court per 1,000 people 1 basketball court per 1,000 people 1 tot lot per 200 people 1 baseball diamond per 2,000 people. 1 softball court per 2,000 people. 1 recreation center per 2,000 people. 10.5 acres of local park land.	n/a
27. Change in perceived pleasantness of recreational experience.	n/a	n/a	n/a
Education			
28. Change in number of students within x minutes walk or y minutes ride from school.	For new students: The 265 elementary pupils would likely have to be bused to nearby schools until new school constructed in area, because of road hazard. Students would still be within 1 mile of school. Junior high students (108) must be bused also. Senior high (97) may walk conveniently to neighborhood high school. Existing students not affected.	Same.	Yes.
29. Number and percent of students having to switch schools or busing status.			

EXHIBIT 10 (CONT.)

| IMPACT AREA | MEASURE | IMPACT ON CLIENTELE GROUPS | | | COMPLIANCE WITH COMPREHENSIVE PLANS |
		Planning Area	Neighborhood—Including Low and Moderate Income Families		
Education (cont.)	30. Change in crowdedness "breakpoints" or indicators; student, teacher, and parent perceptions of crowdedness and pleasantness of schooling.	No change in pupil/teacher ratio or crowdedness even without any new school construction.	Same.		Yes.
Local transportation	31. Change in vehicular travel times between key origins and destinations.	1-2 minute increased delay during peak hours.	*W-L*[1] None calculable.	*Rest of Area* 1-2 minute increased delay.	Note: Physical transport system complies with Master Plan; measures do not apply in terms of "compliance."
	32. Change in duration and severity of congestion.	Negligible. (duration). —————— Slight increase. (severity).	*W-L* None. —————— None.	*Rest of Area* Negligible. —————— Slight increase.	Level of service decreased on local street system, within acceptable range, assuming programmed local and proposed site-related improvements to nearby intersections and completion of Edson Lane.
	33. Change in likelihood of finding a satisfactory parking space within x distance from destination in neighborhood.	No change.	*W-L* Surplus parking.	*Rest of Area* No change.	n/a
	34. Change in numbers and percent of residents with access to public transit within x feet of their residence; and, percent of employees who can get within x distance of work location by public transit.	No change or improved access.	*W-L* 100% acceptable access to transit (within 2,000 ft. of a transit stop).	*Rest of Area* No change.	

			W-L / Rest of Area	
Local transportation (cont.)	35. Change in the rate of traffic accidents.	No change.	*W-L* Rate should be less than average. *Rest of Area* About the same rate.	n/a
	36. Number and percent of citizens perceiving a change in neighborhood traffic hazard.	About the same.	*W-L* Safe. *Rest of Area* About the same.	n/a
	Change in pedestrian usage of streets, sidewalks, and other outdoor space.	Same.	Improved (developer provides overpass & interior bike/hiker paths). About the same.	
Shopping	37. Change in number of stores and services (by type) available within x distance of y people.	n/a	Will provide local stores within 2000 feet walking distance for people in project. No other population likely to use this commercial area.	Yes.
	38. Change in the percent of people generally satisfied with local shopping conditions.	No observable change.		Yes.
V. Housing and Social Conditions Housing adequacy	39. Change in number and percent of housing units that are substandard, and change in number and percent of people living in such units.	No observable change.	No change.	Yes.
	40. Change in number and percent of housing units by type relative to demand or to number of families in related income classes in the community.	197 townhouses. 193 garden apartments of which 36 moderate priced. 295 mid-rise elevator apartments (4-5 stories) of which 28 moderate priced.	Same.	Yes.

EXHIBIT 10 (CONT.)

| IMPACT AREA | MEASURE | IMPACT ON CLIENTELE GROUPS | | COMPLIANCE WITH COMPREHENSIVE PLANS |
		Planning Area	Neighborhood—Including Low and Moderate Income Families	
People displaced	41. Number of residents, or workers, displaced by development—and by whether they are satisfied with having to move.	None.	n/a	Yes.
Population Mix	42. Change in the population distribution by age, income, religion, racial or ethnic group, occupational class, and household type.	Small increase in moderate income residents in homogeneous high-income area.	Increase of 10% in moderate income residents in area of high incomes.	Yes.
Crowdedness	43. Change in percent of people who perceive their neighborhood as too crowded.	n/a	n/a	n/a
Sociability—Friendliness	44. Change in frequency of visits to friends among people in the existing neighborhood after the new development occurs, and frequency of visits between people in the existing neighborhood and the new development.	n/a	n/a	n/a
	45. Change in percent of people perceiving the neighborhood as friendly.	n/a	n/a	n/a
Privacy	46. Number and percent of people with change in "visual" or "auditory" privacy.	n/a	n/a	n/a

Privacy (cont.)		n/a		n/a		n/a
	47. Number and percent of people perceiving a loss of privacy.	n/a		n/a		n/a
	48. Change in percent of people who perceive their community as a good place to live.	n/a		n/a		n/a

NOTES: 1. W-L means Wall-Luttrell, the name of the proposed development.
      2. n/a means not available.
      3. 1-4 DBA causes no impact, 5-10 DBA causes minor impact (according to HUD).

VIII. IMPLEMENTATION: GETTING STARTED

The inertia and barriers to be overcome in getting a new evaluation system implemented can be formidable, especially if one is not prepared for them. This chapter suggests how a local government can decide whether or not to use a comprehensive measurement system, and how to get started. It is partly based on the experience, albeit limited, in trying to get measurement systems tested in the three participating governments. At least two of the three participating governments felt that the process of asking the questions and trying to identify existing tools and data resources justified the initial effort even though the final decision might be to proceed no further with a formalized system.

SHOULD WE GET STARTED AT ALL?

At least four questions should be considered (even if they cannot be answered with complete assurance) before spending much effort on developing a measurement system:

Is There Enough Room for Improvement?

Some governments without a formalized measurement system already do an excellent job of assessing potential impacts of development. If the quality of information available for decision making is rarely an issue, if the government already is using the better state-of-the-art techniques in all impact areas, if consistency in decision making is rarely called into question, if decision makers and staff communicate fairly well on the facts of a case, and if new planning department employees are able to be quickly indoctrinated in the ways to evaluate developments, then there may not be sufficient justification to get started on a measurement system even if it will produce some marginal improvements.

The considerations just cited may be reviewed separately for project reviews and for development of comprehensive plans. Improving project reviews may be less critical if they are undertaken in the context of comprehensive plans, if those plans give major attention to potential impacts, and if the plans are updated frequently. A comprehensive impact measurement system may be used to evaluate alternative plans even if it is not to be adopted for development reviews.

Is There a Clearly Defined Set of Users for the Measurement System?

First of all, is the planning board, zoning commission or other body responsible for reviewing most rezonings likely to welcome improved information? Are they capable of understanding the system, and open-minded enough to benefit from it? If not, the planning staff may still make good use of the measurement system for developing their own comments, though not presenting them in the form and language of a measurement system to the board or commission. If the planning staff itself is not receptive to the use of the system, and their initial hostility cannot be allayed, then

87

there still is potential for use by the zoning administrator or planning director himself, in those decisions for which he personally has decision making powers (often this includes special exceptions and variances), and as a checklist against which to judge the completeness of reviews developed on an ad hoc basis by the staff.

Is There Enough Legal and Political Room for Use of a Measurement System?

As noted in earlier chapters, some states may restrain the considerations allowable for evaluating individual developments. Maryland, for example, with its "change and mistake" rule, considerably limits the factors that can be considered in an individual zoning map amendment. Courts in some other states also have held that fiscal reasons alone, or aesthetic reasons alone, are insufficient to justify the rezoning of a parcel of land. There also must be political room for maneuver. If a balanced consideration of impacts is not likely to get fair hearing because of extreme pro-growth or anti-growth local attitudes, for example, it may be futile to embark on a systematic approach, although one might conceive instances where the systematic approach would be implemented as part of a strategy to help achieve a more balanced communitywide view of growth and development.

Are the Citizens, Courts, and Local Decision Makers Likely to Cause Rigid Use of the Measurement System?

If it is likely that every development will be required to be reviewed in detail by pressures from any of these sectors, it may be preferable not to get started. This may become a problem especially if a measurement system is adopted by ordinance. When legislation required Florida's "Development of Regional Impact" reviews, it was virtually impossible to meet the demands of the measurement system for each case without prohibitive expenditures, or questionable validity on many measures. (The Florida requirements have been modified since their inception, to make them more realistic and more in line with budget allowances for review processes.)

These four major questions may not be answerable before an initial trial is made. But if the planning director, planning commission chairman, or equivalent official feels that this gauntlet of questions can be successfully run, at least in the longer term, it then would be appropriate to look at the means of implementing the systematic impact measurement approach.

SUGGESTED STEPS FOR IMPLEMENTATION

Nine steps are suggested here for implementing the system. There is no special significance to the order in which they are listed.

1. *Identify potential users—especially boards and commissions—and enlist their support.*

The prime users determine in part the form of the measurement system and, perhaps equally important, the amount of resources that can be allocated to its development and use. Some if not all potential users will not be clear on what the system is, how it is used, or what the benefits are, so a firm identification of users may not be possible initially. To gain the early support of the prime decision making body or bodies—zoning commissions, planning boards, and so forth—seems prudent. It is a fact of life that they often determine the priorities of the planning staff. Without their endorsement of the system for their own use or for staff use, it would be difficult to find the time, money, or staff motivation to develop the system and put it to use. If planning staff members do not see eventual use of the system by the decision making body, their disinterest in the system may defeat it before it gets off the ground.

2. *Identify a set of community objectives for land use planning.*

This should not be just a very generalized statement along the lines of promoting the welfare of the community by good planning, or the like, but rather a list, such as illustrated in Exhibit 2, which will identify the major attributes of community life that should be considered in evaluating developments. Some suggestions on how to develop such a set of objectives were given in Chapter III.

3. *Develop a tentative list of impact measures.*

To flesh out a local statement of community objectives with specific yardsticks or measures, an initial starting point might well be the list of suggested measures in Exhibit 3.

Initially the list may be developed with planned unit developments or other multi-faceted forms of development in mind to bring to light the maximum number of impacts to be considered. On the first pass it is well to identify all impacts that you think ought to be considered in decision making, regardless of whether they are currently accepted by the courts or applicable in all situations. This is a useful exercise both because it shows how restrictive the local legal situation is, and because there are many situations—as in the evaluation of alternative comprehensive plans or in informal negotiations with developers—where various considerations come into play beyond those legally acceptable as the prime basis for individual development decisions. Also, the exercise may suggest directions for trying to test or move the courts. On the initial pass, it is useful to disregard data collection problems and costs and simply identify what would be the most desirable measures; later steps take account of the constraints.

4. *Identify measurement needs by decision making purpose.*

Two dimensions must be considered: the type of development review (variances, rezonings, PUDs, subdivision reviews, policy and comprehensive planning, special exceptions, etc.) and the major stages in the review process (reviews by planning staff, planning commission, hearing examiner, appeals to council, courts, etc.).

For example, in Indianapolis, a variance is initially evaluated by the development review section, which presents potential impacts and recommendation to a five-man variance board. The board decides the case. The focus at this stage is on the statutory requirements of a variance, e.g., would it relieve an "undue hardship" of the owner—and not the impact on the community, even though variances can be used for sizable developments. Appeals of the board's decisions go to the development commission (and beyond that to the courts), which would consider a broader range of planning principles in making a decision—including impacts on the community. Thus the breadth of analysis that is applicable changes with the step in the process. In this case, a broadening of view occurs. For some types of reviews, a narrowing takes place. For example, considerations raised in a rezoning hearing often include

citizens' views which would not be allowed by the courts on appeal of the case.

To facilitate review of measures applicable for various decision purposes and stages, a chart such as shown in Exhibit 11 may be used. This form was used in Indianapolis; a similar one also was tested in Montgomery County. For this exercise, legal constraints at various steps should be considered. Participants in various stages of decision making outside the planning staff preferably would be brought in to review the measures at this step, if that has not occurred earlier. The review may be assisted by focusing on specific issues that arose in various steps in the planning process over the past few years to see if the list of issues and measures is indeed reasonably comprehensive. Also, one would check to see if impacts that are not obviously allowable by the law did arise and, if so, whether they were upheld as allowable for consideration.

The classification of measures by type and stage of review should help indicate the priority for developing measures, based on the breadth of their application. Of course, some measures that may be useful at only one stage in the process may still be considered vital.

In Indianapolis, the result of these exercises indicated that the considerations addressed by most measures already have arisen—or had the potential of arising—another in most types of review and at most stages of decision making. Therefore it was felt that a single common list would be preferable to several with minor variations.

5. *Identify available data and data gaps.*

Given a desired list of impact measures, it is then necessary to see whether practical data collection and analysis procedures can be found for each measure. A first crucial step is to identify existing capabilities within the jurisdiction and in higher level jurisdictions, such as state environmental monitoring groups. The desired list of measures can be divided up according to agencies or groups most likely to have the data, models, and in-house analytical capability for generating the necessary information. These organizations would be asked to respond in writing, specifying the scope of the data they can provide and their analysis capabilities. If they are unable to provide the precise data desired they should be requested to identify

EXHIBIT 11
FORMAT FOR REVIEWING POTENTIAL USES OF IMPACT MEASURES FOR VARIOUS TYPES AND STAGES OF DEVELOPMENT REVIEW
(as tested in Indianapolis)

MEASURES FOR EVALUATING THE IMPACT OF LAND DEVELOPMENTS		POLICY AND COMPREHENSIVE PLAN			VARIANCES			REZONING				PLANNED UNIT DEVELOPMENT			SUBDIVISION REVIEWS		
IMPACT AREA	MEASURE	Staff	Policy Commission	Commission	Staff	Zoning Board	Courts	Staff	Hearing Examiner	Commission	Council	Staff	Commission	Council	Staff	Plats	Commission
I. Local Economy																	
Public Fiscal Balance	1. Net change in government fiscal flow (revenues less operating expenditures and annualized capital expenditures).																
Employment	2. Number of new long-term and short-term jobs provided.																
	3. Change in numbers and percent employed, unemployed, and under-employed.																
Wealth	4. Change in property values.																
II. Natural Environment																	
Air	5. Change in level of air pollutants and number of people at risk or bothered by air pollution — a) near the development. b) areawide.																
Water	6. Change in level of water pollutants, change in tolerable types of use, and number of persons affected — by each body of water.																

Noise	7. Change in noise and vibration levels and number of people bothered by excessive noise and vibration.
Greenery and Open Space	8. Amount and percent change in greenery and open space — on the development site itself and in the community.
Scarce Resource Consumption	9. Change in frequency, duration and magnitude of energy shortages (electrical, natural gas, fuel oil), and the number of persons affected.
Natural Disasters	10. Change in number of people and value of property endangered by ...

the closest proxy likely to be available. The responses should also include estimated man-days, out-of-pocket costs, and lead time needed to generate the necessary information. Montgomery County used a form shown in Exhibit 12 for assessing the data available from various groups.

The survey should include information on models available in the community for estimating air pollution dispersion, traffic distribution or movement, flooding danger, and water quality. The level of detail (that is, the size of the area and the unit of time) that can be treated by the models should also be identified, since that influences whether they are suitable for one-by-one reviews, planning, or both. Other information might include skills available, such as whether there are any biologists capable of wildlife surveys; citizen surveys that have been made on either a regular or one-shot basis that relate to neighborhood usage and perceptions; studies of fiscal impacts of different types of residential developments; and so forth. The data might include information on available consultant expertise or local university capabilities as well as purely in-house resources.

To emphasize the point, the information survey should include departments other than just the local planning department. Widespread anecdotal evidence suggests that development review and even long-range planning do not always make full use of capabilities in other municipal departments. Planning departments do not always have full, up-to-date information regarding the models or expertise that exist in other departments in their jurisdiction, and they in turn do not always fully appreciate what the planning department needs. The explicitness of the measurement system may help serve as a communication vehicle to smoke out the necessary information.

The exercise of identifying data sources was found to be extremely worthwhile in itself by at least one of the participating jurisdictions in this study. Often in day-to-day activities analysts in various parts of the government are asked to provide information on potential development impacts but are not asked about the quality of the information or what untapped resources exist.

The resulting picture of the community's capabilities probably will reveal information gaps important to know about for other than just development review purposes. It also allows a basis

for estimating the start-up and continuing costs for undertaking evaluations at various levels of detail.

6. *Select measures and measurement procedures.*

Based on the critiques obtained from the various departments given an opportunity to review the initially suggested measures, the existing data resources, the resources available for filling gaps, and an idea of the potential community of users and breadth of use of the various measurement areas, some initial decisions can be made on the measures to be included in the measurement system, proxies or fallback measures feasible under the various constraints, and the data collection and analysis procedures that can be used for this set of measures.

The measurement procedures that will be used should be documented. This will improve the ability of all potential users to understand what the data really means and something about its reliability. Having the data collection procedures documented also will prove to be a significant benefit to new members of the planning staff who will participate in project review and evaluation of plans. Some planning directors see a major benefit of a documented measurement system as a training guide—another side benefit that may accrue from even informal use of a measurement system.

7. *Make initial trials.*

The now tentatively defined measurement system should be tested using an actual development case. Preferably, this would be done using both the new approach and the previous one simultaneously, for comparison of benefits and estimation of the difference in costs and time, but this dual approach may not be feasible where the same small staff would have to do both versions. More frequently, two types of tests may be feasible. A development already reviewed may be reviewed again using the measurement system, seeing how the data developed could be converted into the end-oriented measures, what impact areas were omitted altogether and might have been caught, and perhaps most importantly, making a judgment as to whether the final decision would have been different or reached sooner or made more palatable if the expanded measurement system had been available. A single case will not

EXHIBIT 12

ILLUSTRATIVE EXCERPTS FROM FORM USED TO EVALUATE POTENTIAL
MEASURES AND IDENTIFY DATA SOURCES
(Montgomery County, Maryland, 1975)

Measure	Applicant for Proposed Development Approval Supplies this Information	Commission Has Access to this Information or a Substitute Indicator	Department or Agency which Has Access to this Information	How Useful Is the Indicator? How Difficult Is it to Measure?
13. Views blocked, degraded or improved.	—	Yes, through site plan.	Development Review Division and Urban Design.	Useful in the sense of a general observation—not in terms of numbers. Can be measured by empirical study—requires time and resources—may not be cost effective.
14. Visual attractiveness as rated by citizens and experts.	—	Citizen information *not* available except as some individual statements in hearing transcript; could be obtained through survey. Expert staff opinion can readily be generated in-house.	Development Review Division and Urban Design.	*From Citizens:* Not very useful—tends to be subjective—judgment will tend to be negative due to general aversion to any additional development. *From Experts:* Indicator can be readily measured using generally accepted design standards. Indicators are of questionable use due to unwillingness of courts and decision makers to consider aesthetic judgments as argument either *for* or *against* development.
15. Change in neighborhood attractiveness as rated by citizens.	No	Information *not* available—could be generated through surveys or transcript of hearing. Experts could rate change in neighborhood.	Obtainable by Montgomery County Planning Department through survey.	Indicator not particularly useful—indicates subjective judgments and usually reflects general discontent to almost any change in neighborhood character (except in extreme circumstances). Indicator of questionable use in judging for or against development.

EXHIBIT 12 (CONT.)

Measure	Applicant for Proposed Development Approval Supplies this Information	Commission Has Access to this Information or a Substitute Indicator	Department or Agency which Has Access to this Information	How Useful Is the Indicator? How Difficult Is it to Measure?
IV. *Public and Private Services—Recreation*				
25. Change in the number of people within – or beyond – x miles or y minutes from recreation facilities by type of facility.	Anticipated number of housing units and/or population. Parkland acreage and facilities to be supplied by developer.	Determine relationship between anticipated population of development to proposed open space and/or facilities in terms of current open space and facilities standards.	—	This will indicate whether or not the development will provide adequate community open space and facilities for its residents. This can be accomplished with moderate staff time.
26. Change in usage as a percent of capacity; waiting times, number of people turned away; facility space per resident; and citizen perceptions of crowdedness at recreation facilities.	Anticipated number of housing units and/or population. Parkland acreage and facilities to be supplied by developer.	Determine net change in parkland and/or facilities adequacy for population and facilities within ½ mile of proposed development and/or within planning area.	—	This will assess the impact on surrounding parkland and facilities if there is a net surplus or deficit in development supplied parkland & facilities. This will require substantial staff time to prepare on a project-by-project basis.
27. Change in perceived pleasantness recreational	No	None	None	This parameter cannot be obtained without ongoing user/attitude survey.

tell the whole story, but a few cases might give good insights.

A second "quickie" test is for the zoning administrator or planning director, members of planning boards, zoning commission members, or the person in charge of a particular development review to personally use the measurement system qualitatively—on the side, so to speak. Then, in the course of a few actual proposal evaluations, they can see if it leads to different questions, improves consistency or speed of analysis, and so forth.

8. *Decide and disseminate.*

Based on the various studies and initial tests, a decision must be made whether to proceed with the system on a trial basis and, if so, whether to use it informally for staff use only, or to use it more explicitly for presenting results to the decision makers. For a level of use other than informal private use by a few individuals, some training and discussions will be necessary. Emphasis should be on the purpose of the system, how it is to be used, how it is not to be used, the definition of the measures and measurement procedures, and assignment of responsibilities for reviewing developments of various types and for developing models or procedures to fill information gaps.

We think that it may take several exposures to the concept of an impact measurement system before it is communicated reliably even to professionals in planning staffs and top management.[1]

Until then many fears may be raised along with challenges to the concept. It is especially necessary to communicate the flexibility of the system and its potential usefulness at various levels of available resources (staff time, expertise, and funds).

9. *Evaluate the system.*

It is usually difficult to assess the value of additional information, especially in land use decision making where political pressures play a key role. After some initial trial uses of the measurement system, the planning director at the minimum should review the quality of the development reviews in terms of comprehensiveness, clarity, likely reliability, and usefulness in the decision making process. If a change has been made in the way information is presented to the decision makers, they too should be surveyed to see if they feel there is an improvement in the quality of the information obtained: Have they been able to reach a decision with greater ease and confidence? Does it provide them with a better basis for defending, explaining, and justifying their decisions (an issue that is sometimes forgotten)? The apparent improvements must then be weighed against the costs of providing the information to see if the system should be pursued, and if so at what level.[2]

---

1. This communication problem seems to arise because there are so many related concepts and terminology in use that it is hard to find the vocabulary to distinguish one from another reliably.

---

2. We would appreciate hearing from any governments that are willing to share with other jurisdictions information about their experiences with measurement systems. Summaries of such experiences may be sent to the Executive Director, Land Use Center, The Urban Institute, 2100 M Street, N.W., Washington, D.C. 20037.

IX. ASSESSING THE APPROACH: LOCAL OFFICIALS SPEAK

As noted previously, three local governments assisted in testing the use of impact measurements during the course of the study: Phoenix, Arizona; Indianapolis/Marion County, Indiana; and Montgomery County, Maryland. The nature of the testing in each case was different due to local circumstances and varied local assessments as to the likely benefits from the proposed approach.

In Phoenix, measurement checklists were tried out by (a) the Zoning Administrator, personally, in deciding on zoning adjustment requests; (b) the planning staff as background for preparing comments on rezonings for the consideration of decision makers; (c) the planning commission as part of the development of policy and plans (the measures help sharpen questions and encourage a comprehensive outlook; and (d) citizens as guidance for their participation in planning advisory groups.

Indianapolis carried out several of the initial steps toward implementing a measurement checklist, including the identification of measures and available data sources and discussion of the concept with the planning staff and planning commission. It also tried the checklist evaluation approach on a few brief test cases (summarized in Chapter VII).

Montgomery County also undertook an initial identification of measures and available data, followed up by an assessment by the planning staff of the merits of the approach. A detailed test case was developed (described in Chapter VII).

This chapter summarizes the assessments, by planning officials in each of the three communities, of the apparent usefulness of using a comprehensive impact measurement system for evaluating development. The Phoenix conclusions and impressions are discussed in somewhat greater detail because of the more extensive application there.

The results, as will be seen, were mixed. Some considered the approach to have potential usefulness for present application, others did not. There was strong consensus among the three governments, however, on one point: that further improvements of practical procedures for assessing various types of impacts are needed, and that the recommended approach will gain in usefulness as more reliable procedures for assessing a broader range of impacts become available. Perhaps the primary difference in opinion centered on the weight to be given to those types of impacts which are difficult to assess with confidence, and the extent to which these hard-to-measure impacts should be explicitly considered or reported as part of development reviews. Although personal judgments possibly account for some of the divergencies of opinion, the different viewpoints more likely stem from the widely varying legal and institutional environments of the three jurisdictions and from the distinct development issues of importance in each location.[1]

---

1. It should be stressed that what did *not* seem to be a factor in the different responses to the system was the willingness of the three governments to consider new approaches. On the contrary, each has been actively pursuing the reshaping of its development review and planning process under able leadership and competent staffs.

97

Below we summarize the assessments of the suggested impact evaluation scheme by the planning director (or equivalent position) in each of the three communities. Wherever possible their own words are paraphrased or quoted directly. Our own overall assessment of the advantages and disadvantages of the system was given in the Summary and Recommendations section at the beginning of the report. It does not seem appropriate to draw a single, generally applicable conclusion. Each local government can best decide, on the basis of the pros and cons of the system, whether its particular decision making climate in respect to land development is likely to benefit from use of the measurement checklist.

PHOENIX EXPERIENCE AND CRITIQUE
By Rick Counts, Zoning Administrator [2]

The checklist approach to development impact analysis is applied selectively in Phoenix. That is, most planning decisions are not understood as requiring deep, multi-faceted analyses of the facts presented. Some development proposals, however, are sufficiently complex or involve so large an area or so strategic a location as to warrant detailed testing of potential impacts.

Various written checklists have been used in these "testing" instances, ranging from recent adaptations of The Urban Institute's 48-point analytical framework to an environmental impact matrix. Ordinarily, selective cost-benefit measures are applied to those cases which raise public controversy and, therefore, require the consideration of positive versus negative development effects. It is relatively common for a development proposal to raise questions involving six to eight of the 48 measures; those involving a third or more of the criteria are rare; and none, to date, has required full evaluation on all or substantially all of the 48 identified checks.

Phoenix's use of the checklist takes two distinct forms: Staff-infused evaluation and "self-administered" evaluation. In the former case, the selected impact assessment topics are identified by staff, researched and computed, and incorporated into staff recommendations. Such staff recommendations are prepared for decision makers (i.e., Planning Commission—which recommends approval or denial, and City Council—which, of course, has final decision making authority) on cases involving requests for rezoning, zoning ordinance text amendment, site plan appeals, subdivisions, lot splits, alley vacations, appeals under the sign ordinance, and the like. "Self-administered" criteria are applied by individuals, such as the Planning Director or Zoning Administrator, who are charged with making interim or final decisions for certain zoning adjustments (e.g., variances), use permits, and certain zoning appeals. In these cases, instances where formal staff reports are generally not required, the decision maker's own use of the checklist is particularly important to consistent, well-reasoned results.

It is anticipated that utilization of checklist evaluations will increase substantially, both in terms of the number of cases affected as well as in evaluative accuracy, when refinements of measurement procedures become available.

Checklist Application Toward Legislative Decisions: Rezonings

The preponderance of cases in which the Planning Commission and City Council have been exposed to checklist criteria are those which have involved major requests for rezoning. Through staff recommendations, Council and Commission members receive analyses of such potential impacts as: traffic congestion, incidence of flooding, fiscal balance, employment, aesthetics, and population mix. Although many of these cost-benefit comparisons had been incorporated within staff recommendations in the past, *there now appears to be an increased breadth of perspective*—"Have the effects on employment been considered?" "What about the natural desert landscaping?"—*both on the part of staff and the decision makers.*

During 1974–75, Phoenix was faced with several critical land development proposals. Three in particular [3] involved more than 1,000 acres each and represented significant departures from the City's "1990 Comprehensive Plan." These pro-

---

2. The italicized portions of Mr. Counts' critique are views from the test community selected for emphasis by the author of this report.

3. The Arizona Biltmore Estates, Village of Paradise Valley, and Desert Springs applications.

Using An Impact Measurement System

posals were eventually approved by the City Council after lengthy study, comment, and a series of public hearings held by the Planning Commission and Council; but each was considerably modified from its initial, proposed form as a direct result of impact evaluations raised by elected and appointed officials, staff, and citizen participants.

While it would be erroneous to say that the checklist was the primary approach used in evaluating these projects, it can be said that the *analyses were aided by staff use of the checklist to identify impacts which might require further investigations.*

Checklist Application Toward Administrative Decisions: Zoning Adjustments

Decisions made by administrative personnel rely upon the individual's own impact evaluation within the predetermined bounds of his or her office, whereas the filtering process involved in reaching legislative development decisions—staff review, Planning Commission recommendation, and City Council action—adapts impact analyses into a context of broader political and economic reality.

Zoning adjustment decisions (e.g., variance or Use Permit actions) are made, in Phoenix, by the Zoning Administrator—with the right of appeal to the Board of Adjustment. These cases rarely affect land development to the extent rezonings change the configuration of the neighborhood or the entire city; nonetheless, similar kinds of judgments—balancing costs against benefits—are required. In zoning adjustment matters the requested relief, by law, must be found "not materially detrimental" to the area in which the subject property is located. This test patently demands that the anticipated positive effects of development are measured against the negative effects, with an approval of any application resulting only from an affirmative finding.

At one time or another, over the course of approximately 1,000 adjustment matters heard in a year, nearly all of the 48 checklist points can be applied. Some, of course, are more frequently relevant than others. Criteria dealing with availability of services, housing conditions, and aesthestics often impinge directly on the test for potential detriment. Less frequently, questions of

environmental impact are germane to the assessment of the applicant's request. Economic considerations—which are explicitly ruled out as determinants in variance cases—may sometimes be applied indirectly, as, for example, where construction of new offices under a Use Permit application may benefit the area by encouraging improvement of nearby properties.

The Zoning Administrator is both gatherer and user of impact data. Information on each case is provided through staff research and on-site inspection as well as through the testimony of the applicant and any other interested persons appearing at the public hearing. Prejudgment is avoided—the weighing of the various factors raised must be done at the time of hearing.

Typical zoning adjustment illustrations of impact analyses include: potential traffic hazards; air, noise, and water pollution factors; protection of views and privacy; aesthetic considerations, such as landscaping, setbacks, and site plan designs; property security; accessibility to public and private services; and a full range of private property rights as balanced against public welfare concerns. A high incidence of cases, nearly 25 percent, involve structural expansions which usually raise the countervailing questions of increased housing adequacy (more room for a growing family) versus conditions of crowdedness (e.g., inadequate setbacks or excessive lot coverage) and possible reductions of neighboring property values.

Testimony may be heard as follows: "We moved out there for the Western lifestyle. Being able to hear the coyotes at night in the desert adds to our enjoyment of our property. The proposed development will drive off the native Arizona animals." This is typical of the varied elements which have to be considered in zoning adjustment cases. Or one hears: "There's too much parking on the street in our neighborhood. Those apartments should provide an adequate number of spaces on their property so the kids won't be playing around parked cars on their way to school." Or: "We've had several instances of vandalism in the past year—I'd feel more secure with a six-foot fence. . .be able to sleep at night." Contra: "A high, chain-link fence in the front yard would be unsightly; it would detract from the neighborhood. . ."

Although the Zoning Administrator does not decide cases with a checklist in front of him, tracing his finger from one pertinent impact test to the next, *the comprehensive perspective gained from a "checklist awareness" does contribute to a more thorough consideration of all issues* which may be raised by a citizen's request. In particular, *consistent use and understanding of analytical tools encourages a greater breadth of pre-hearing research—investigation into not only the obvious consequences of a proposed development but, more importantly, into potential issues,* any one of which might have a bearing on the decision, and *which might otherwise be forgotten.* Identification of these additional points of inquiry, to be noted and discussed with the applicant and other interested parties, is one of the major values of the checklist. Frequently, *the cumulative weight of impact checks which may have been regarded as of only secondary importance can bring about modification or reversal of an initial decision-reaction.*

Too, on matters appealed to the Board of Adjustment from a decision by the Zoning Administrator, the checklist exercise can prove extremely worthwhile. *Where case findings are based on several explicit, factual considerations rather than on a single, general impression, the reasonableness of the prior judgment is more apparent—and the likelihood of reversal is decreased.*

Checklist Application Toward Policy/Advisory Decisions: Planning Commission Recommendations

The Phoenix Planning Commission, in its role of advisory body to the City Council on planning and zoning matters, has become increasingly cognizant of the need to account for various types of predictable development impacts. As discussed above in regard to Commission recommendations to Council on rezoning, members are familiar with the assessments in staff reports of development proposal implications. Commissioners, further, have their own copies of The Urban Institute report on the impact measurement system.[4] *They often raise additional impact criteria in hearing a case—directing questions to staff*

or the applicant to probe further into one or another of the checklist measurements.

Recently, the Commission demonstrated its pragmatic concern for cost-benefit data by examining a citizen planning group's presentation of a recommended community area plan in heretofore unheard of detail. This emphasis, at least in part, may be attributed to the Commission's acceptance of impact analysis techniques.

The Commission has recently begun an intensive Urban Form Directions study, addressing eight urban growth subject areas through the deliberations of staff-supported citizen committees. Each of the more than 200 citizen participants has been provided a copy of the initial Urban Institute report on impact measurement. Preliminary goals reports from several of these panels appear to incorporate a respect for the realities of plan implementation—again, at least partially ascribable to the present reminder of evaluation criteria. The Land Use Subcommittee of Urban Forms Directions recommended that:

> . . .The Urban Institute publication, *Measuring Impacts of Land Development,* be used as a guide in determining appropriate measures for evaluating the impacts of land developments. At a minimum, the following impact areas should be used: (1) public fiscal balance, (2) views, (3) recreation and education, (4) local transportation, (5) air and noise pollution, and (6) storm drainage. To obviate the need for redundant data collection for each development proposal, and to reduce developers' costs in preparing applications, the committee recommends that the city develop a data base on all impact measures and make that data base available to developers preparing impact reports.

Conclusion

The City of Phoenix is experienced in weighing land development proposals. To preserve the qualitative values in urban decision making, however, it is evident that analyses must become increasingly perceptive and sharp.

Impact factors have traditionally been accounted for within Phoenix's system for arriving at land use solutions. Now, through the tentative introduction of The Urban Institute checklist at various levels within the process—citizens, staff,

---

4. Schaenman and Muller, op. cit.

Commission, Council—the need for measured evaluation is being recognized. Better, the checklist approach may soon become institutionalized, understood, and specifically tailored to the city's own, unique characteristics.

Finer impact assessment calibrations—as they become available through research or by way of local refinements in measuring devices—are expected to *provide a comparative base for establishing development precedent.* And for continuing, modifying or overturning precedents as cumulative impacts approach established, acceptable development intensity thresholds. *Rather than dictate policies or predetermine decisions, an impact measuring process that can be applied by elected decision makers can verify the accuracy of gut reactions—now that too much is at stake to continue to fly into urban growth by the seat of our pants.—Rick Counts*

INDIANAPOLIS CRITIQUE

The utility of an impact measurement system was assessed quite differently by different parties to the land use decision making process in Indianapolis.

The *Planning and Zoning Subcommittee* of the Development Commission indicated that a measurement system was not likely to be very helpful for individual development reviews, even for informal use as a personal checklist for members.[5] Evaluations were considered to be already systematic and comprehensive, and the members carried the equivalent of a checklist in their heads. They did not like the idea of more data requirements leading to more staff work, increased costs, and potentially longer hearings. They did not agree with the notion that in the long run a systematic approach might save time or make it easier to understand what was different about each case relative to others. They also did not react positively to the notion of a consistent evaluation approach; they argued that each case has to be looked at from its own perspective, and did not see this as equivalent to dealing with a subset of the measures most relevant to the particular case.

The chairman of the subcommittee did, however, feel there could be merit in applying the system to the planning process, and seemed interested in the possibilities of relating comprehensive plans to the one-by-one decision process via targets or thresholds for which running tabulations would be maintained for a particular measure.

The *planning staff* had mixed reactions to the project. One concern was voiced by some staff members who were often called on to supply information for reviews in addition to their main planning roles, but were not part of the development review section. They felt that their workload, which was already heavy, could increase further if a measurement system was used explicitly, since it might lead to increased requests for information and was unlikely to decrease any, without necessarily improving the decisions at the end of the process. They also raised a question: If currently supplied information was not fully used in the political decision making process, what justification was there for more?[6]

The planning staff members directly responsible for development review seemed generally positive toward use of a measurement system, at least for use internally by the staff. They felt it offered the potential for somewhat more comprehensive reviews "to make sure we aren't missing anything significant," especially a collection of non-obvious impacts that together might be significant. They felt it also facilitated more consistent review from case to case, using the measurement checklist at least as a common starting point regardless of who had responsibility for a given development review. They noted that a checklist might have saved them some embarrassment in at least one case—Example 1 in Chapter VII—in which localized air quality and noise impacts led to citizen demonstrations and passing out of handbills at the city/county building in protest.

The Director of Planning and Zoning, F. Ross Vogelgesang, summarized their collective views on the impact measurement system as follows:

We feel that the checklist is of the most value to the staff to serve as a reminder of the many impact considerations involved in each

---

5. These opinions are the author's interpretation of comments made at a presentation by F. Ross Vogelgesang, Director of Planning and Zoning, to the Planning Commission on November 14, 1974.

6. This same question was raised by planning staffs in many communities.

case. We can use it to demonstrate to petitioner and other parties that we do have a thorough and consistent approach to case analysis and preparation of staff comment. We can use the checklist as a training tool for new employees in both planning and zoning, and to assure continuity of procedure through frequent changes in staff personnel.

Our attempt to use the checklist on specific cases has demonstrated the unavailability of pertinent data in both our department and other agencies to support many points in the outline. If data is available it is rarely in a form which can be readily used by the staff. It appears that we have a tremendous job before us to devise a system for recording pertinent information in a manner suited to the needs of the Development Department. Until that can be accomplished, the planners will have to simply dig out information on a case by case basis.[7]

One concern we have with regard to developing an elaborate system for data storage is that in many cases such detailed information is not warranted and our expenditure of time is not justified. Perhaps trial and error will help us to devise a better approach or improve judgment on when a detailed analysis is warranted.

While we are optimistic about the use of the guidelines by our staff, we do not believe they will be used by Board members, Commission members, or Council members unless specifically directed to do so on a case by case basis. Although the outline is in reality simply stated, it is still too sophisticated for use by these other people.

It does, however, give us something to work toward. Perhaps (in the future). . .and with the initiation of more formal training sessions, we should be able to call their attention to the importance of such a process.

---

7. Indianapolis attempted to identify data sources as an early step toward testing the practicality of a measurement system. Somewhat less capacity to supply the necessary data was uncovered than had been expected. This may have occurred partly because of the reliance development reviewers must place on the in-house experts who respond to their ad hoc requests for information.

MONTGOMERY COUNTY (MARYLAND) CRITIQUE

The Montgomery County planning staff already uses many advanced impact analysis techniques, especially in the areas of natural environment and fiscal impacts. Exhibit 10 (Chapter VII) illustrates types of data that are already available for the potentially more significant developments. They are continually adding to their repertory of analytical tools as ones that are proven practical become available. Because implementing new tools typically requires a start-up fund, new techniques tend to be added one at a time as funds are approved. Recent additions include models of demographic, fiscal, transportation, stormwater drainage, and air quality aspects. Noise assessment techniques also were being planned.

On the question of whether a formalized measurement system would be useful and cost-effective for project reviews, the planning staff consensus was that, at least at present, the institutionalization of the total checklist would *not* be appropriate. The following statement by the Montgomery County Planning Director outlines their rationale.

Statement on System by Planning Director Richard Tustian

It was the concensus of the planning staff who worked on this project, including myself, that any formal requirement for staff to include a rundown of the entire checklist in all rezoning and subdivision and special appeal cases does not seem warranted at present. There are a number of reasons for this conclusion, all of which are best understood in the context of the present comprehensive planning, zoning, and subdivision process.

The various facets of this total process have been outlined in our 1974 growth policy report, entitled *Framework for Action,* as well as in several recent newsletters and papers of the American Institute of Planners. The most relevant aspect for this discussion of impact measurements is the fact that the Montgomery County growth management system places heavy emphasis on a planning step that is intermediate between the general plan for the county and the individual project review.

Using An Impact Measurement System

This intermediate step is called the community plan or the area master plan covering subareas of the county and analyzing them in considerable detail. Depending on geographic boundaries, the subareas of the county allow for population units that range in scale from about 10,000 persons to as high as 100,000 persons. In general, these areas do not have local self-government, so the County Council is the decision maker for planning, zoning, and subdivision over nearly the entire 500 square miles of the county.

In the past, these community plans have been of the traditional "end-state" character, showing the desired layout of public and private land uses without regard for the design of the intermediate stages prior to the area reaching full development. Over the past five years, we have been trying to develop the idea of "staged" master plans, which would incorporate instructions for maintaining a design balance between private sector growth and public facility growth at various intermediate stages in time. The points in time are measured ordinally, rather than cardinally, in terms of a series of "trigger points," which are described in terms of the completion of certain public facilities and/or the completion of a certain amount of residential-commercial growth in different areas. The plan prescribes that when the trigger points are reached, the plan itself should be monitored and reassessed as a formal action, to determine if it needs amendment. A further extension of the same principle of updating is the Planning Commission's program effort to maintain an official reassessment of all these master plans within an approximate ten-year cycle.

In the development of these plans, as much impact assessment as is possible within the state of the art and the budget limitations is performed. Currently, this includes the quantitative estimation of such functional elements as traffic and transit, water and sewer, storm water and air quality, housing and employment, and parks and other public facilities, as well as estimated cost and revenue projections. Thus, the concept of including both "staging" and "impact measurement" into the master plan is intended to provide a way to perform impact measurements in as sophisticated a manner as possible, but at as low a public cost as possible. The presumption is that it is more effi-

cient in terms of the use of technical staff to conduct the impact measurements at the scale of the master plan than it is to conduct them at the scale of many more and smaller project reviews. In addition, the use of the master plan as the vehicle of impact measurement "balance" allows for the necessary trade-offs that must be made among competing functional elements, which sometimes are at variance with each other in terms of optimization. The scale of the master plan allows an opportunity to blend such inconsistencies into a composite judgment.

Obviously, it takes time to complete a full set of such master plans; and because conditions and knowledge are constantly changing, the job can never be finally complete. Consequently, even with this emphasis on the master plan as the vehicle for impact measurement, the necessity to process a constantly flowing stream of individual project reviews requires a method of handling those projects which fall in areas that do not have one of the new generation of master plans. In our situation, this problem is alleviated by two factors.

The first is that the county has already adopted a set of first generation "end-state" master plans for all the important growth areas of the county, and in addition has an adopted statute that prevents the County Council from adopting an individual zoning map amendment contrary to a master plan recommendation unless it achieves an extraordinary vote of 5 to 2, or is accompanied by a recommendation of approval from the Planning Board. The second is that the Maryland Court of Appeals over the years has developed something called the "change and mistake" rule, which has had the effect of permitting the county to refuse to accept individual zoning map amendments unless the applicant can prove there has been a "change in the character of the neighborhood" or a "mistake" in the original comprehensive zoning allocation performed when zoning was first introduced into the county.

The combination of these two factors, coupled with an aggressive and well-funded planning program have tended to reinforce the significance of the master plan in the decision making process. It has also tended to shift the county from being in a reactive position, with respect to individual zoning map amendments brought by private property owners, to more of a leadership position in terms of laying out in advance the kind of development that is desired. The latter, of course, is accomplished through the master plan, but also through the increasing use of what is known as the "sectional map amendment," which is a large-scale rezoning initiated by the county government. A sectional map amendment is not limited by the "change and mistake" rule of the courts and must only be held to be "reasonable," "non-arbitrary" or "non-capricious." The courts have also held that "floating zones" are permissible, which are "non-Euclidian" zoning categories initiated for application by the landowner and which are in the nature of a "special exception." Floating zones by definition include a set of performance criteria which have to be demonstrated as being adequate in order to obtain the rezoning.

With the above brief description of the planning process in mind, let us return to the question of whether it would be desirable to formally institutionalize the entire checklist that has been developed by this Urban Institute study. To properly answer this question, it is necessary to examine the relevance of the checklist to each of the major points in our process, namely, the master plan, the individual zoning map amendment for euclidian zones, the individual zoning map amendment for floating zones, and the sectional map amendment.

In the case of the individual zoning map amendment process for euclidian zones, we believe that it would be wasteful and ineffective to require all staff reports to formally identify each of the steps in the total checklist. Primarily this is because the "change and mistake" rule, as well as the statutory requirement for conformance to master plans, together constitute the overriding criteria that tend to govern in the case of a court challenge. No matter how attractive a project might be on the basis of other criteria in the checklist, a zoning map amendment to higher density can be overruled by the courts on the basis of the "change and mistake" rule and has, in fact, been so done in the past. On the other hand, if a project appears unattractive on the basis of certain criteria in the checklist and yet is still in accordance with the adopted master plan, then the county government is in a difficult position to argue in court that it

should not be granted unless they are willing to show that the master plan itself is defective in this respect. This has occasionally happened in our stiuation where master plans are very much out of date, but the court test requires a rather hard set of data and quantitative analyses such as appear to be possible within the present state of the art for only a very few of the total set of criteria in the checklist. The further problem in using the total checklist in this case would be the probability of generating public confusion. The formal use of all the items in the checklist would suggest to the uninformed lay public that these criteria are, in fact, permissible and desirable in the decision making process. For the government to then have to turn around and explain the limitations on their use in each and every case seems inefficient.

In the case of individual zoning map amendments for floating zones, the zoning text description of permissible uses in each zoning category must incorporate a statement with regard to the kind of criteria upon which each individual application will be judged. Some of these are relatively broad, using terms such as "compatibility," and others are quite detailed, using such specific criteria as decibel ratings at the lot line, etc. Thus, in the case of a court test, the admissible criteria are limited to those which can be proven to have direct relevance and relationship to those stated in the statute. Because each of the zones is a little different in this respect, we do not believe it would be fruitful to administratively institutionalize the entire checklist as a requirement to be described on each and every project, regardless of which floating zone category it fell into. In this sense, our staff uses the "organic"/preplanned tools approach of describing and quantifying for each project in this category as many impact measurements as seem reasonably consistent with the text of the zoning in question. The example of a planned development zoning proposal used in this Urban Institute study [Chapter VII, Example 4] represents the kind of information that is generated by such a process.

In the case of the sectional map amendment, initiated by the government to cover a large area as well as a number of different zoning categories, any court test of its validity will, under our planning system, go back to examination of the master plan. Consequently, the use of a checklist for sectional map amendments is, in fact, redundant.

In the case of the master plan, there is a local statute that spells out a process by which plans are to be prepared and developed. This process establishes the necessity of the County Council approving the initiation of the plan as well as a series of documents along the way that range from a concept document in the beginning, through a preliminary and final plan, all of which are subject to public hearings and participation. The amount of impact measurement that goes into each of these plans is a function of the state of the art and the available budget. To some extent, the available budget determines the state of the art in the sense that impact measurement requires an investment in research and quantitative techniques and simulation models. Because our process allows for public examination and Council determination of the kind of impact measurements that are brought into the master planning process, we do not believe it would be fruitful to officially require that the entire checklist of criteria developed in this study be formally addressed in each plan. Although conceptually we have no problem with the idea of expanding the number of impact measurement criteria that should be brought into the master planning process, we have in the past been forced to recognize the shortage of funds, and the imprecision of certain measurement techniques, as real constraints on the amount that can be done by staff.

An additional problem has been raised by our legal staff, who have observed that any official institutionalization of a required checklist of impact measurements in the master plan preparation would subject the Commission to a variety of law suits brought by any number of individual citizens, who could charge that the particular impact measurement had not been performed correctly, or in sufficient detail. The possibility of a wide number of such law suits could appear to pose a significant threat to the ability of the county to continue producing master plans within any reasonable time frame commensurate with the needs. In addition, of course, would be the public expense involved in such litigation.

The one category of project review that I have not mentioned thus far is the public facility project. Here the application of the checklist

would seem like a useful addition to the regular decision making process inasmuch as it would assist the public officials to be more aware of the impact of their proposals, and yet at the same time would not be subject to the impediment of externally generated law suits. Again, however, if all of the checklist criteria were made an official requirement, the problem of how to handle suits alleging inadequate exploration of any specific functional element would have to be dealt with.

In summary, for the reasons stated above, the planning staff did not feel the entire checklist developed by this study should be formally required at any of the points within our total process. The four major reasons for proceeding cautiously are the limitations on the state of the art, the limitations on the budget, the limitations on citizens' understanding of the processes, and the potential problems of excessive litigation. Having said this, however, let me also very clearly express that the kind of work that has gone into this pioneering effort by The Urban Institute is, in our opinion, extremely valuable. A research study of this kind which systematically examines the range of impact measurements, as well as the state of the art for each, is a wonderful contribution to existing knowledge. Our staff feel that this report, in particular the sections that examine the techniques with regard to each of the checklist elements, constitutes a very important contribution to the planning process generally and provides the basis from which the further institutionalization of practical measures can be developed in the future. We intend to use it ourselves and we trust that it will be of value to others also in a wide variety of circumstances.—*Richard E. Tustian*

CONCLUDING STATEMENT

Each local government must judge for itself whether to use an impact measurement system either formally or informally for any or all aspects of its evaluations of land use changes, proposed or past. The decision must be reached in light of the jurisdiction's own legal, financial, and political circumstances, its available staff, and the current state of the art. The decision is not a simple one. As exemplified by the three jurisdictions whose judgments are spelled out in this chapter, quite different conclusions may be reached by competent, professional, and conscienious officials.

We hope this report and others in this series will assist governments to reach decisions on impact measurement that are appropriate for their own particular situations. As we have made clear throughout the report, we are still a long way from the last word on evaluation methodology, so we also hope this work spurs the development of improved techniques and approaches.